READING ON!

developing reading at Key Stage 2

EDITED BY DEE REID AND DIANA BENTLEY

© 1996 Diana Bentley, Dee Reid, Suzi Clipson-Boyles,
Jenny Monk and Sylvia Karavis

Published by Scholastic Ltd
Villiers House
Clarendon Avenue
Leamington Spa
Warwickshire CV32 5PR

1234567890   6789012345

Authors Diana Bentley, Dee Reid, Suzi Clipson-Boyles,
Jenny Monk and Sylvia Karavis
Editors Dee Reid and Diana Bentley
Sub-editor Angela Thomas
Series Designer Lynne Joesbury
Designer Toby Long

Designed using Aldus Pagemaker
Processed by Pages Bureau
Printed in Great Britain by Bell & Bain Ltd, Glasgow

The right of Diana Bentley, Dee Reid, Suzi Clipson-Boyles, Jenny Monk and
Sylvia Karavis to be identified as the Author of this work has been asserted by
them in accordance with the Copyright, Designs and Patent Act 1988

British Library Cataloguing-in-Publication Data
A catalogue record for this book is available from the British Library.

ISBN 0-590-53430-0

PRIMARY
PROFESSIONAL BOOKSHELF

CONTENTS

PRIMARY

PROFESSIONAL BOOKSHELF

ACKNOWLEDGEMENTS

Valerie Bloom and **Cambridge University Press** for 'Chicken Dinner' by Valerie Bloom from *Duppy Jamboree* by Valerie Bloom © Valerie Bloom (1992, Cambridge University Press).
Gina Douthwaite for 'Five Haiku' from *Let's Celebrate* © 1989 Gina Douthwaite (1989, Oxford University Press).
Anne Franks-Fond, Basel, Switzerland for the use of an extract from *The Diary of Anne Frank*, translated by B. M. Mooyaart, (first published in Dutch 1947, 1953, in English).
Murray Pollinger for permission to use an extract from *The Witches and the Singing Mice* by Jenny Nimmo.
Walker Books Ltd for an extract from *The Mousehole Cat* by Antonia Barber and Dawn Bailey © 1990 Antonia Barber and Dawn Bailey (1990, Walker Books) and from *The Stone Mouse* by Jenny Nimmo © Jenny Nimmo (1993, Walker Books).

PREFACE

Pupils should be encouraged to develop as enthusiastic, independent and reflective readers. They should be introduced to a wide range of literature, and have opportunities to read extensively for their own interest and pleasure and for information. Pupils' reading should be developed through the use of progressively more challenging and demanding texts.
English in the National Curriculum Key Stage 2 Reading

Pupils reading fiction will increasingly encounter texts of some complexity in plot, relationships, language and structure. The teacher will offer varied approaches: reading aloud to pupils; group reading; providing access through drama. Poetry will encompass a wider range of styles... With informational texts, teachers can now help pupils recognize how texts dealing with different types of knowledge differ... It is important to recognize that the form of assessment has to match the aims of the teaching/learning process... it is important for the pupils to know and share what is to be learned, including the criteria for assessment.
English Language 5–14 Reading Level D.

Teachers should continue to encourage pupils to enjoy reading and provide opportunities to extend the range of their reading experiences. Enjoyable learning is fostered in a reading environment where curiosity is aroused, interest is generated and a sense of achievement is assured. Teachers can build on pupils' enthusiasm by offering a range of texts.
The Northern Ireland Curriculum: English Key Stage 2 Reading.

INTRODUCTION

Once children have mastered the skills of reading adequately and choose to read silently many teachers are very uncertain how to develop their reading further. Some schools colour code the class library according to the perceived difficulty of the texts; others use a published graded scheme; others encourage children to choose for themselves from the school or class library. The danger with any of these approaches is that the emphasis may be on reading more and more rather than ensuring that the children develop as critical and reflective readers. Too many children develop only as surface readers. These children read for the story alone and rarely explore such subtle aspects of a text such as making inferences and sophisticated deductions about the plot and characters.

The reading demands of the curricula upon pupils between the ages of Year 3 – Year 6 are enormous. The majority of children entering Year 3 are able to read and understand the following text:

> 'There is dust on your chairs,' said Frog.
>
> 'Tomorrow,' said Toad.
>
> 'Your windows need cleaning,' said Frog.
>
> 'Your plants need watering.'
>
> 'Tomorrow!' cried Toad.
>
> 'I will do it all tomorrow!'
>
> SAT Level 2. Lobel, A. (1992) *Days with Frog and Toad*
> (Heinemann).

To be able to read the above successfully, children need to recognise the words, distinguish between the two characters and understand the relationship between them. The text contains a lot of repetition, direct speech and short sentences all of which are closer to spoken language and therefore easier to read. At Level 4 children are expected to read the following silently.

> Malcolm stood by Mrs. Cooper's desk with his matchbox.
>
> His contribution was definitely the most interesting thing

that anyone had seen that morning. He was only sorry that
he hadn't seen it himself.

An excerpt from the short story by Jan Mark, *The One that Got Away*, taken from the SAT KS2 Reading Assessment Booklet *Getting Away from it All* (Crown copyright 1995).

This text not only requires the reader to read the lines but to also infer what has happened, to recall what had happened on a previous occasion and to unravel the intricacies of the plot.

Helping children to move from being readers of *Frog and Toad* to being a reader of *The One that Got Away* requires a careful structured reading policy. In order to achieve Level 4 of the National Curriculum children should be able to:

• infer appropriate meanings;
• challenge assumptions within and about the text;
• interpret characters, setting and plot;
• classify the kind of text they are reading;
• evaluate the success of the text;
• respond on a personal and critical level.

The chapters of this book address the range of reading that is required at Key Stage 2.

HOW THIS BOOK IS ORGANISED

CHAPTER 1 – DEVELOPING THE READING OF FICTION

This chapter considers a range of approaches to teaching fiction including the importance of reading aloud, the benefits of group reading and the place of solo reading.

CHAPTER 2 – DEVELOPING THE READING OF NON-FICTION

This chapter considers the range of text types found in the genre of non-fiction and describes their characteristics. It looks at the challenge posed when reading non-fiction and describes ways to help children to become familiar with the range of different genre.

CHAPTER 3 – DEVELOPING THE READING OF POETRY

This chapter examines the nature of poetry and suggests ways to develop children's reading and response to all forms of poetry.

CHAPTER 4 – TEACHING READING THROUGH DRAMA

This chapter explores how a range of texts can be enhanced through drama and how this can deepen children's understanding.

CHAPTER 5 – A MULTI-MEDIA APPROACH TO TEACHING READING

This chapter looks at the huge range of texts found within different media forms and it presents a case for using a variety of media for developing children's reading.

CHAPTER 6 – ASSESSMENT

This chapter looks at assessment beyond the standardised reading tests, and at ways to integrate assessment into the reading cycle. It considers the value of assessment through observation, individual reading interviews and self assessment.

CHAPTER 1

DEVELOPING THE READING OF FICTION

This chapter looks at the various conditions and opportunities that should be offered to children in the Junior years to develop their reading of fiction. It considers the importance of reading aloud to children, benefits of group reading, and ways to extend children's solo reading. For each of these areas ways are suggested to develop children's responses to and reflection upon their reading so as to achieve their more sophisticated comprehension. In this chapter particular emphasis has been given to the importance of the teacher reading aloud to children. This is because in the reading aloud situation a teacher can model the skills which are to be developed in children and explored in group reading and absorbed into silent reading.

As teachers we know what we want children to be able to do eventually with the reading skills they acquire in school. We want them to be able to process and interpret all kinds of texts swiftly, to absorb information efficiently and to select information appropriately. These skills are invaluable, especially in a world dominated by technical forms of communication. Apart from such practical uses of reading, we also want children to discover in works of fiction new ways of interpreting life; to come across new language with which to encode life's experiences and to enjoy that special 'other-worldliness' that can happen when we read.

The literary theorist, Wolfgang Iser, charted the relationship between a reader and a literary text. He argued that for some of the time when we are reading we are conscious both of ourselves and of the characters portrayed in the book. There are, however, also periods of time when we read when our involvement is so powerful that we may actually inhabit the world of the text. We identify with the characters so closely that we celebrate their joys and share in their grief. We are no longer thinking that these are imaginative constructs, the creation of some author. The characters are as real to us as members of our own family. This is the power of fiction to present us with plausible realities – a secondary world in which all seems 'true'. We use expressions like 'lost in the book' to explain how our normal consciousness of everyday things grows dim and the more powerful reality is the characters and actions of the book.

Many adults are familiar with this experience and it is an aspect of the reading process that we would like children to experience, but it is also the least tangible skill to be taught in the busy classroom with children at various different stages of reading ability.

> The National Curriculum (1995) requires that children at Key Stage 2: '...should be encouraged to respond imaginatively to the plot, characters, ideas, vocabulary and organisation of language in literature'.

These are challenging demands and, if we sense that much of what Iser was writing about implied a private and solitary act undisturbed by others, then it seems unlikely that we could replicate the conditions for it to occur in the classroom. As teachers we need to give children models of how to make a range of responses to fiction; we need to give them opportunities to explore response, both in groups and individually. We cannot just tell a child to 'get lost in a book'. This can only happen when the reader feels unthreatened in terms of his or her ability to decode the text. When a reader is constantly breaking out from the world of the book to recognise an unfamiliar word, the likelihood of the book conjuring up an alternative world is very slight.

This should not, however, lead us to suppose that children cannot respond to stories at all levels – emotional, psychological and cerebral – before they have completely mastered the skills of reading. We have only to picture the absorbed features of Infants at story time to realise that we do not have to be the reader of a book in order to enter its fictional world. The experience can be just as powerful if we hear the story being read to us.

READING ALOUD TO CHILDREN

Teachers have always known that it is important to read aloud to children. With the pressures of the National Curriculum, however, it can be very difficult to ensure that this is a regular and extended experience for all children.

The National Curriculum places emphasis on children reading from a wide range of literature and developing their reading through the use of progressively more challenging and demanding texts. One way to raise children's interest in a range of genre and to tempt them to read adventurously, is to read aloud to them.

Some teachers who already. spend time reading aloud to their classes may not be aware of the benefits that it can bring to their pupils; others may see it first and foremost as a relaxing time when the teacher does the work and the class 'just listen'. Such sessions can be more than enjoyable experiences with books (although that in itself is a real achievement for some children) if we use it as a time to lay down the foundations of how, as readers, we make contact with the world of the book.

Many of the skills of responding to literature are impossible to model when the text is read just by an individual child. We would need to have comprehensive knowledge of every book chosen in the classroom and the time to allow the individual to reflect slowly upon how the book is affecting them. Few classrooms offer the luxury of this span of time spent by a teacher with an individual pupil. These skills can, however, be taught to the whole class when the text is read aloud by the teacher and heard by everyone.

Teachers can provide a model for all those higher order reading skills that Primary Language course books struggle to recreate. We can model three levels of response for children from Roger Beard's *Developing Reading 3-13* (1990):

◆ reading the lines (following the plot);
◆ reading between the lines (drawing out inferences and assumptions);
◆ reading beyond the lines (generalising and speculating).

Many children get stuck in their development as readers once they have mastered the decoding skills. Their word recognition skills are quite good but they need the opportunity to develop the skills of understanding the meaning behind the words on the page. Children who, at an earlier stage of their reading development, may have been quite sensitive to irony when sharing picture books where the humour derives from the ironic distance between the picture and the text, often fail to develop these skills further when the reading consists solely of text.

Reading aloud offers children a shared literary experience that heightens the possibility of children becoming absorbed in the story. The mere fact that it is a common experience raises its importance. Children enjoy talking about television programmes that they have all seen and if they have shared the same story experience then understanding is deepened through the informal chatter and the more formal discussions which surround the story.

BOOK CHOICE

The decision to read a particular book to a class comes only after some careful deliberation. How the final decision is reached provides considerable learning opportunities: we do not always think to share these deliberations with the class but they could become a model for helping children to make more effective choices of books for their own private reading. A teacher chooses a book after having considered these issues:

1. **Length of time it will take to read to the class**: This, in turn, is affected by how familiar the class is with the procedure of listening whilst a story is read aloud. This is a learned skill and one which some children find difficult to acquire.

2. **How well the teacher knows the class**: Some books raise issues which are best discussed when the teacher and the class

are settled comfortably together.

3. The amount of time available: Timetable decisions have to be made about the allocation of time spent on reading aloud. Some teachers build it in as a short daily routine; others work around a more extended weekly experience. This, in turn, might affect the choice of book chosen to be read.

4. The content of the book: There may be particular reasons for reading certain books. These may revolve around curriculum needs. A book may:

◆ link thematically with an on-going topic

◆ raise a particular issue that is relevant to the children at that time

◆ be by an author with which the children are familiar/ unfamiliar

◆ be from a specific literary genre to which the teacher wishes to introduce the class.

5. Books for boys and books for girls?: Much of children's private reading in the Junior years divides along gender lines with boys predominantly choosing the fast-paced action stories and the girls preferring the more reflective, psychological stories. Some books, of course, appeal to all in an age-group and some children enjoy a very eclectic taste in books. The dilemma facing the class teacher is to choose those books to read to the whole class which will not be seen by either gender group as an example of a 'boys' book' or a 'girls' book'. One way to avoid this is to increase the amount of reading aloud that goes on in the classroom. If only one book is read per term then either the boys or girls can be justified in feeling that their first interests are not being considered. If, however, a book which might, **on the surface**, seem to appeal more to the girls is only one of ten titles read aloud that term, then the class can be more understanding. The greatest challenge is to find those books (and they do exist!) which appeal to the whole age-group and which have enough action to appeal to the boys and enough reflection to appeal to the girls.

6. Choice of genre: Choice of book may be based upon its genre. For example, we might want to share some historical fiction with the class as this provides a further dimension to reading around a history topic. All of the considerations which are taken into account by a teacher when choosing a book, can be part of a class discussion. It is important that children realise the constraints upon choice or scope for choice. Successfully choosing books for private reading presents enormous problems to all but the most avid child reader and if, as teachers, we share some of the decision-making with the class this can help to develop those skills.

As a general rule, it is advisable to choose to read aloud to the whole class stories that are not already the most popular choices for private reading. If we read to children those stories that they may well have opted to read voluntarily, then we are missing an opportunity to extend their range of reading. Reading aloud sessions offer an opportunity to share texts which benefit from adult mediation and interpretation. This does not mean that we should choose obscure or particularly difficult books to read aloud but rather to read those titles which do not grab the reader on the first page, or stories which take some time for their magic to unfold. It is worth remembering that when we choose a book to read to the whole class we are, in some respects, endorsing the values portrayed in that book and so we should choose wisely.

Of course, the range of reading specified in the National Curriculum should also be reflected in the books we choose to read aloud. The reading aloud slot is the perfect opportunity to introduce significant children's authors and to read some long-established children's fiction. This usually benefits from adult help to clarify what might be old-fashioned language and to cope with the different sentence constructions which characterise those texts.

A list of suggested titles of books suitable for reading aloud can be found at the end of this chapter on pages 38 to 40.

ACTIVITIES BASED ON CHOOSING BOOKS

Book titles: Read out the titles of a number of books to the class and ask them, first to discuss with a partner and then to share as a whole class, suggestions about the whole of the book based on its title. Encourage awareness about different kinds of titles: titles which are the name of the main character (e.g. *The Story of Tracy Beaker*); titles which reveal something important about the main character (e.g. *The Owl Who was Afraid of the Dark*); titles which give the name of the main character and an important object (e.g. *Martin's Mice*); titles which name several characters (e.g. *Emil and the Detectives*); titles which name an important object in the story (e.g. *Flour Babies*); titles which use play on words (e.g. *The Celery Stalks at Midnight*).

By increasing awareness of the significance of titles we can alert children both to author style and to features of the book's genre. Once a book has been chosen, it is worth referring to its title from time to time during the reading to make connections between the title and the text. Children can become more sensitive to aspects of genre which are often indicated by the title of the book.

Book openings: Read out opening sentences from a range of different books. This activity not only gives children writing ideas when they are writing their own stories but it also draws attention to the genre of the book and the style of the author. Initial clues about either of these features are often subtly conveyed in the opening sentence of the story and we need to raise children's awareness of this. On occasions we can read out opening sentences without having first alerted children to the title of the books. Encourage them to make predictions about the genre from just the opening lines. For example clues about fantasy genre are evident in the opening line of Tolkien's *The Hobbit* (HarperCollins): 'In a hole in the ground there lived a hobbit'. Philip Pullman's historical melodrama, *The Ruby in the Smoke* (Puffin) opens: 'On a cold, fretful afternoon in early October, 1872, a hansom cab drew up outside the offices of Lockhart and Selby, Shipping Agents, in Cheapside.' The school genre is evident in the opening sentence of *The Turbulent Term of Tyke Tyler* by Gene Kemp (OUP): 'We'd gone right through the school canteen collecting the teachers' tea money and had got to the canteen door when Danny waved the ten-pound note at me.' The opening lines of *It shouldn't happen to a Frog* by Catherine Storr, published by Piccolo, immediately set the scene for a re-worked fairy tale: 'If I'd been the princess in that story, the *Frog Prince*, I wouldn't have thrown him against the wall.'

Story openings provide clues to the plot and introduce the genre. It was Roald Dahl whose dictum it was to grab child readers on the first page or risk losing them forever. He knew the importance of story openings particularly for young readers who can so easily be put off reading. If we can make children more aware of what kind of story is going to ensue and what the author is trying to do with a story opening, then we may help to reduce some of the feeling of strangeness and uncertainty that children sometimes experience when first dipping into a book.

Continuing in the style of the author: To extend this exercise in recognising the genre of a book, read the opening line of a story and then ask the children to work in pairs to write the next line of the story. This forces them to be sensitive both to genre and to author style.

Matching titles and openings: Choose four fiction titles and write out the opening lines from each. Show children the titles of the books then read the opening lines out to them. Ask them first to discuss and then to decide which opening lines go with which titles. Encourage them to reflect on how they made their decisions.

THE SKILL OF READING ALOUD

When a suitable book has been chosen to read to the class, we can also share with children the decisions surrounding how we intend to deliver the text. For example, you may have decided to abridge the story and only to read selected sections to the class. Share with the children **why** you have made this decision and **how** you are going to achieve it. Will you need to write linking sections between the original text to maintain continuity or will you do this spontaneously as you read?

Ask the children to consider why you have chosen a certain way of presenting a character. Has this been your choice alone or has the author indicated in the plot how a character speaks? Perhaps the clues about how to present a character are evident in the way the text is written on the page with dialect written phonetically.

When we read aloud to children the author's/narrator's voice becomes more evident. In private reading, however, children may be aware of the spoken voices of the characters in the text, but they may not be conscious of the 'other' voice in the story – that of the author/narrator. When reading aloud it is almost as if we personify the author's voice and children who may never previously have been aware of the fact that there is a voice in the book over and above the character's voices may, for the first time, sense an author's presence. Teaching awareness of this point can be very beneficial when helping children to develop as writers: many children write excessive amounts of dialogue in their own stories because they have not realised that their voice as author must also be present.

MODEL REFLECTIVE READING

As you read to the class, re-enact the role of the interactive reader by posing questions and making predictions. Too often we are tempted to do the reading ourselves and then test the children's listening capacity by asking them questions which require factual recall. Sometimes when we read aloud to children and we are tempted to discover how well the children have listened we ask closed questions. For example, the following passage comes from the opening of Chapter 2 of *The Stone Mouse* by Jenny Nimmo (Walker Books).

'It's a dirty old pebble,' said Ted, sliding down the banisters.

'Ted, don't do that,' said Mrs Martin, climbing past him.

'Mouse!' said Ted. 'Elly's crazy.'

Ted is dangerous, thought the stone mouse.

Elly scowled at her brother. Sometimes he just wasn't worth talking to. She picked up the stone mouse. He was soft and silky with bright, dark eyes and very small ears, but he had no tail at all.

Too often we are drawn into asking such questions as:
1 What was Ted doing to annoy
a) his sister?
b) his mother?
2 Describe the stone mouse

Instead we could demonstrate for children the running commentary that goes on in a reader's head as they make sense of the text. For example: Ted is obviously in a bad mood otherwise why call it a 'dirty' old pebble? He is saying that to annoy Elly and he's sliding down the banisters to annoy his Mum. Why is he so out of sorts? What kind of stone mouse is it if it can decide that Ted is dangerous? In what sense do I think that Ted is dangerous and what will this mean in the rest of the story.

If children are to appreciate what goes on in a reader's head, we need to make overt all the processes we go through to sort out the plot and any confusions. We need to show children that it might be the author's intention that we are confused at any particular stage of the story. Most inexperienced readers assume that if there is any confusion, it is their own inadequate reading skills which have caused it. As adult readers we know that any 'mysteries' in the text will eventually be explained to us if we persevere. Children, with less reading experience, may be inclined to abandon the book believing it to be too hard for them. They fail to recognise that some uncertainty is a deliberate ploy on the author's part. The idea that an author might manipulate the reader for dramatic effect, may not have occurred to them. When children watch television programmes they are adept at picking up all the clues in the plot upon which the plot hinges. They know how to interpret even an apparently casual glance between two characters. Yet, not all children look for these same clues when reading. We can stop from time to time when we are reading aloud to children to question such things as 'Do I believe that character when he says that?', 'What is the author making me feel about that character by describing her in that way?', 'What is going on now – I'm a little confused?'.

ASKING OPEN-ENDED QUESTIONS

To encourage children to reflect as they listen to the story, prepare some open-ended questions for everyone to consider. It is important to prepare such questions as they are difficult to think up on the spur of the moment and it is all too easy to fall back on factual recall questions which are much easier to snatch from the air.

Some examples of open-ended questions:

1 Do you believe what the character has just said? If not, why not?

2 Has anything like this ever happened to you?

3 Do you feel the same about the character now as you did at the beginning of the book?

4 Does this book remind you of another book you have read or programme you have watched?

5 Through whose eyes do you see the action of the plot?

Encourage children to discuss their answers to these questions with a partner before sharing answers with the whole class. In this way, all children have the opportunity to respond, even those who might be hesitant to do so in front of the whole class.

The oral nature of all this response is very important. There will be some children in the class whose only experience of hearing stories well read will be in your reading aloud sessions. Their own reading skills are insufficiently developed for them to hear the stories in their heads as they read silently. This does not necessarily mean that they are weak at responding when someone else is doing the reading. These weaker readers have no opportunity to show in their writing that their skill at response is developing if their writing skills lag far behind their reading skills. It can be a considerable boost to these children's self-confidence if they realise that they are as good as the next child at responding to reading.

HELP CHILDREN TO PICTURE AND IMAGE
AS THEY LISTEN

Research from America (Nanci Bell, 1989) has highlighted the importance of readers visualising as they read. She describes the importance of making generalisations as follows: Some readers 'When they read or listen, they often grasp a few facts but get lost after a few sentences. This means that they can recall a few specifics but cannot generalise and create a 'whole' or 'gestalt' from the information. They get 'parts'.

In the process of visualising we make generalisations as we read and these generalisations help us to form the images.

Images are much easier to recall than text and so our comprehension of what we read is directly affected by the amount we image as we read. As we image we draw inferences based on what we have read and in this way we interpret the story both as author's words on the page and in the light of our own life's experiences. All readers will re-create in their minds images conjured up by the author's words but each image will be slightly different, depending upon personal experience. The French literary theorist, Roland Barthes, says,

> That is what reading is: rewriting the text of the work
> within the text of our lives.

Some children may have poor visualising skills or even be unaware that other readers visualise as they read (after all, there is no overt sign of visualising going on in the silent reader!). When we read aloud to children we can share with them some of the visualising we are doing as we read and encourage them to share theirs. Tony Martin in his book, *Readers and Texts in the Primary Years* (1994), asked children:

'What can you see now? With whose eyes can you see this happening?' In this way he helped children both to recall in visual terms and to identify with characters in the story.

Louise Rosenblatt in her book, *The Reader, the Text and the Poem* (1978), considers picturing and imaging as the first level of response when we read. So, if some children are finding even this difficult, they are going to find other levels of response impossible.

ACTIVITIES TO HELP CHILDREN TO VISUALISE

Presenting the images in shapes and colour: Some children will enjoy turning the pictured images into artwork and this can be a satisfactory way to encourage imaging. There are children, however, who might feel that their limitations as illustrators would preclude them from portraying the image on paper. It might be appropriate for these children to choose either a colour or a selection of colours to depict their response to a story at any particular point. This visualised response could be further defined by producing the colours in patterns. Are straight-line patterns appropriate, or swirly confused patterns, zigzag patterns or smooth waves? Responding at this level can help children to summarise how they are feeling at any particular moment in a story. Of course, comparisons between the choices of colours and the arrangements of the patterns could be the subject of discussion.

Analogising and fantasising: From time to time in the reading ask the children to reflect upon a scene just read and recall together as much factual detail as possible. For example: 'Where was the table in relation to the door? How many chairs are in the kitchen?' This kind of picturing is usually known as analogising. When you have scoured the text for information provided by the author, ask the children to share their own images conjured up by the descriptions. For example: 'What colour is the back door? What kind of chairs are in the kitchen?' This kind of picturing is usually known as fantasising.

ACTIVITIES TO DEVELOP CHILDREN'S INVOLVEMENT

Response sheet: Photocopy a passage from the story and glue it on to a sheet of A3 paper with plenty of space around it for children to make comments. Ask them to work in small groups and to write a commentary of their responses directly related to any point in the text. These remarks can be questions: 'What does this mean?' or surface level comments: 'Our dog does that too!' or deeper level comments: 'They shouldn't do that. It's bound to go wrong.'

Story structure: Give the class a model of story ingredients, for example: characters; setting; plot; sub-plot; complication; reflection; resolution. When reading aloud encourage children to be aware of these ingredients. Ask questions related to story structure such as: 'Is she a main character or a minor character? How has the setting changed in this chapter? This is the complication of the story – predict how it will be resolved. How satisfactory is the resolution? Are all loose ends tied up? Did it end the way you wanted it to end?' This gives children a language with which to discuss story structure and it will be beneficial when they are doing their own story writing.

'Gaps' in stories: All texts have gaps which, as readers, we fill with our own speculations. The author does not describe every moment of a character's life and sometimes we only learn what a character must have been doing from something that the character says later on. Some gaps in stories we are all likely to fill with similar details. For example: 'This must have happened, even though the author has not specifically told us because now this has happened.' These are usually plot-based gaps. Other gaps in stories which are either description-based or character-based we are much more likely to fill in with details drawn from our own personal lives. When children are writing their own stories they often fail to leave anything to the reader's imagination and this can result in too much emphasis on the insignificant. A typical example is the child who writes a story about a walk in a dark wood but the first three pages describe the child getting up having breakfast, etc. Helping children to see how authors have built gaps into their stories, either for readers to fill or simply because we do not need to be told that information, can help with story writing.

Making text-to-text connections: Much of what we understand when we read is interpreted in the light of other reading that we have done. Even quite young children will make comments like: 'This is like another story I know.' This text-to-text connection (or intertextuality) helps us to interpret what we read. Some children in the class will have had little opportunity to develop a range of texts to draw on to make these connections so we can forge these links for them. By comparing and contrasting characters and events between books we can come to a fuller understanding of each story. Picture books like *The True Story of the Three Little Pigs* which present the familiar traditional tale from the point of view of the wolf can help children to appreciate how our understanding of one book influences our interpretation of another.

SUMMARY

Reading aloud to children gives teachers the opportunity to role model all aspects of reader response. It enables the teacher to involve children in making choices about the books they listen to; to make decisions about the method of delivery and to draw on their understanding of the story with exploratory questions and activities.

GROUP READING

Research into the benefits of group work has shown that if children are given the opportunity to share ideas and discuss their learning, this facilitates their acquisition of new concepts. There are a variety of ways in which group reading can be organised in the classroom. Although the group size is dependent upon the availability of multiple copies of stories, a comfortable working group is of 4-6 children who read aloud the text without the teacher necessarily being present. Children can elect to read sections of text but usually it is divided fairly equally between the readers.

> Without the interaction with others children cannot internalise new skills and only after a skill has been internalised can it be carried out independently. *Group Work in the Primary Classroom,* Maurice Galton and John Williamson (Routledge, 1992)

Familiarising oneself with new ideas in the light of previous experience and using everyday speech enables learners to move forward. When coming to terms with ideas, themes, issues, and concepts in books children need the opportunity to explore them through their preferred form of communication – speech.

> When children bring language to bear on a problem within a small group their talk is often tentative, discursive and uncertain of direction... the intimacy of the context allows this to happen without any sense of strain. In an atmosphere of tolerance, of hesitant formulation and of co-operative effort the children can stretch their language to accommodate their own second thoughts, and the opinions of others. They can float their notions without fear of having them dismissed. (Bullock, 1975)

In many Junior Schools reading has become predominantly a private pastime. This custom of individual reading arose in reaction to earlier approaches which employed whole class reading almost exclusively. Teachers became dissatisfied with the whole class reading approach and sought to replicate reading opportunities more akin to adult reading habits. This move has been welcomed by most schools but it is possible that by concentrating upon private reading we may be losing opportunities for children to deepen their understanding of what they read by talking about it.

The National Curriculum prescribes that children respond to and interpret texts; small-group reading can fit very comfortably into a programme which includes reading aloud to children and private reading.

THE BENEFITS OF GROUP READING

1. Group reading extends reading comprehension. When children have shared a text together they can sort out any possible misunderstandings that may have troubled an individual reader.

2. Children working together in a group can also reach deeper interpretations of a text than might be possible in private reading. The mere fact that different children will hold slightly different opinions will help them to realise that any judgements about characters will have to be tempered in the light of how other readers react.

> As children read, they are involved in a constant, often unconscious, sort of running commentary on the book. Indeed, this kind of response is an integral, inseparable part of reading. ...Each child's response will be unique – a product of his or her unique interaction with the book.'
> *Hooked on Books*, Chris Lutrario and John Hook, (Collins Educational).

3. Group reading gives children a real reason for reading aloud and it allows them to practise skills that often become redundant as they become silent readers. In the group, for the benefit of an audience, they can practise reading with pace, intonation and modulation.

4. Group reading enhances reading motivation. When reading privately, children can easily be discouraged from persevering with a text that troubles them, either because it is too difficult or because it raises issues that they have not come across before. With the support of the group to tackle the less familiar words and with whom to share the puzzles thrown up by the text, children can come to understand how rewarding a challenging book can be.

CLASSROOM MANAGEMENT OF GROUP READING

Successful group work arises out of careful planning. Children need to know exactly what is required of them in the group situation. When roles are clearly established then management of the group is easier. It might be easier, initially, if the group composition is decided by the teacher. Later on, however, when the children are more familiar with group reading, it may be possible for different groupings to be arranged.

POSSIBLE GROUPINGS

1. Self-selected friendship group
2. Mixed ability teacher directed group
3. Mixed/single sex group
4. Similar ability group

Some children will thrive best in certain groupings but it is best to keep a record of the group compositions so that children experience a variety of situations.

GROUP SIZE

The number of children in a group may be determined by the number of copies of the book available but large groups – over eight pupils – are rarely effective because the opportunity to participate occurs too infrequently. In a small-scale research project in Berkshire, teachers discovered that a group of four children was the most effective (Diana Bentley and Anne Rowe, Reading and Language Information Centre, University of Reading, 1991). With a group of this size the opportunity to read occurred frequently and it was a good number to sustain discussion without any child feeling over-awed. Interestingly, the less confident readers preferred a group of six. Presumably this was because each reader's turn came around less swiftly and they were able to hear more of the story read aloud before they had to read aloud themselves.

Within a group children can decide how much reading each participant will do. It is not essential that everyone reads exactly the same amount. Some children enjoy reading aloud whilst others, who might enjoy the group support, prefer not to be responsible for reading too much text aloud. Obviously one has to keep an eye out for the dominant child who would do all the reading given half a chance or the shy child who would avoid doing any reading.

WHEN TO DO GROUP READING

Some teachers have opted to incorporate group reading into the timetable by sacrificing one or two of the quiet reading or Uninterrupted, Sustained, Silent Reading (USSR) sessions per week. This seems a very appropriate time as it is still a reading activity but one that offers different reading experiences to young readers. It is difficult to imagine how children would have the opportunity as described in the National Curriculum, to share reading and develop their response to literature, if they only read privately.

It is possible for the whole class to be divided into groups and for the teacher to move between the groups offering support where necessary. This does, however, have resourcing implications for the number of sets of books available. Also some teachers may feel more confident introducing group reading with one group at a time whilst other children continue with private reading.

SELECTING SUITABLE BOOKS

Books chosen for group reading should not be too difficult for any member of the group. Although children will offer each other considerable support with decoding any textual difficulties this is not really the best use of the group reading situation. The priority in group reading is for the text to be read fluently and comfortably with the stress on following the meaning of the story. Suitable texts therefore are those with subject matter that prompts discussion and which are slightly easier to read than the typical book being read in private by the group members.

An obvious starting place for group reading would be plays published for Juniors. Such texts avoid any problems about who reads what. It is true to say, though, that there is a dearth of good plays **with small cast lists** suitable for Junior readers.

STORAGE OF GROUP READING BOOKS

Once a set of books has been collected for the purposes of group reading it is helpful to keep these resources together. Keeping sets of two, four or six titles together with an elastic band will ensure that individual copies are not lost in the general reading stock. Labelling the books with a sticker to denote the fact that they are a group reading resource reminds everyone of their purpose. Some teachers may choose to keep other linked resources, such as a list of discussion questions, with the set of books. Similarly, those teachers who choose to follow-up the reading with writing tasks may prefer to keep books, questions, writing tasks and pupils' work together in a document wallet.

EXTENDING THE READING INTO DISCUSSION

The purpose of group reading is to share a text and then to share interpretations and responses to that text. In order to do this children need to pose and answer questions before, during and after reading. These questions need to be open-ended and require the children to make personal responses as far as possible. These questions will encourage children to:

✦ develop an awareness of features of the text specific to its genre;

✦ make contacts between their own life's experiences and those described in the book (life-to-text links);

✦ make links between the book and other reading experiences (text-to-text links).

It can be helpful if a teacher (or another adult) is present on the first occasion that a group tackles the questions. The adult should not pose the questions but rather takes on the role of a group member and respond as a reader. Obviously this is only appropriate if the adult is familiar with the book! The adult can provide a model of how to answer the questions which are thought-provoking and reflective and to which there are few, if any, right or wrong answers. If children see an adult struggling to put into words exactly the effect that a book has had upon them, they come to realise the nature of making a personal response to a text.

Aidan Chambers in his book, *The Reading Environment* (1991), asks how people become thoughtful readers:

How do they shift from being pastime consumers of print into being attentive readers of literature? My experience as a reader and as a teacher tells me that one of the answers lies in the kind of talk people do about their reading. Some kinds of talk, because they cause us to think more carefully, more deeply about what we've read, have the effect of making us more aware of what is happening to us.

A list of generic questions suitable for all books is provided below.

SUGGESTIONS FOR HELPING BOOK DISCUSSIONS

General questions:
✦ What kind of book did you think this was going to be?
✦ Have you read any other books like this one?
✦ Could this story really have happened?
✦ Who was telling the story?
✦ Were there any parts you particularly liked/disliked?
✦ What will you tell your friends about this story?
✦ Did the story remind you of anything that you've done?

Plot questions:
✦ What happened first in the story?
✦ Did you guess the ending?
✦ Did you like the ending? How would you have liked it to end?

Time and setting questions:
✦ When did the action of the story take place?
✦ Where does the story happen?
✦ Would you like to visit this place?

Character questions:
✦ Which character did you like most/least? Why?
✦ Do you know any people like the characters in the book?
✦ Who would you most like to meet from the story? Why?

Attitudes in the book:
✦ Who are the most active characters – boys or girls?
✦ Which characters come out best in the end?
✦ Does the author use stereotypes of race, colour or age?

EXTENDING THE DISCUSSION INTO WRITING

Although reading a text and engaging in a focused discussion about it can be an educational challenge in its own right, there can be occasions when the reading and the talk lead quite comfortably into guided writing tasks. The National Curriculum specifies the range of writing that children should experience and an effective way to address this requirement is to write in response to reading. Writing evolves naturally out of talking (which is the first opportunity for learning) and the book itself provides guidelines for the kind of writing that might be appropriate. For example, if children have read a story and explored through discussion the feelings of a range of characters in the story, it is a relatively easy step to move on to write about events in the story from the point of view of a particular character. Or, if the children have considered a relationship between two characters, they would probably feel in control of the writing task if they were to write some dialogue between those characters which is not included in the story.

A list of possible follow-up writing activities is provided below.

WRITING ACTIVITIES TO FOLLOW GROUP READING

✦ Devise a 'Wanted' poster for a character in the story.
✦ Write a diary entry for a character.
✦ Write an acrostic poem based on a character's name.
✦ Write a school report on a character.
✦ Write a newspaper report about an event in the plot.
✦ Revisit a character one year after the end of the story.
✦ Draw a map of the location of the story.
✦ Conduct an interview with a character.
✦ Send a postcard to/from a character.
✦ Defend the 'baddy' in a court of law.
✦ Think up ten questions you would like to ask a character.
✦ Write a conversation between two characters which is not written in the book but which must have taken place.
✦ Devise a board game based on the events of the plot.

ll in Identikit details for characters.

ake an incident in the story and write it as a play script.

Vrite about an event in the book from a different point of
w.

Find five problems in the story and write their solutions.

ASSESSMENT THROUGH GROUP READING

All significant aspects of assessment of reading at Key Stage 2 are dealt with in Chapter 6. It is, however, worth considering specific features of developing reading that can be assessed effectively in group work.

SPEAKING AND LISTENING

Range:
+ explore, develop and explain ideas;
+ share ideas, insights and opinions;
+ read aloud skilfully.

Key skills:
+ show clear and confident expression;
+ make exploratory and tentative comments;
+ make reasoned and evaluative comments;
+ listen carefully;
+ identify the gist of an account;
+ deal politely with opposing points of view.

READING

Range:
+ have opportunities for shared reading.

Key Skills:
+ consider in detail the quality and depth of what they read;
+ respond imaginatively to plot, characters and ideas;
+ use inference and deduction;
+ evaluate texts as they read.

DEVELOPING SILENT READING

Despite the overwhelming benefits of children sharing reading with the whole class and in groups there is still an important place for solo reading in the Junior years. The ability to become engrossed in a text without adult mediation or the support of a group of peers is a skill that all children of this age-group need to develop.

When children read individually they have a measure of freedom over what they read and the skill of choosing books appropriately needs considerable practice. Fulfilling reading experiences depend upon successful book choices and too often children make poor choices. In addition to the considerations mentioned earlier on page 27 children need to consider the difficulty a book may represent in terms of the complexity of language or ideas.

Children also need to be aware of the genre of the book so that they make their book selection based on certain expectations of that genre. For example, a mystery story will require the reader to follow clues throughout the narrative and these clues will culminate in a full explanation of the events at the end of the story.

In order to make a successful choice for themselves children need to know:

✦ the difficulty of the book;
✦ the genre of the book.

JUDGING THE DIFFICULTY OF A BOOK

In some classroom libraries or school libraries children are given guidance regarding the difficulty of books on the shelf by colour-coded stickers. These serve to indicate to any potential readers the approximate level of difficulty of the text. Some teachers and schools prefer, however, not to restrict children's reading habits in this way because they recognise that difficulties in texts are more complex to judge than just noting vocabulary range. A child who is very familiar with a particular subject, for example, horse riding will have considerably more motivation to read a 'difficult' book about ponies than a simpler book about flowers. Also, if the children's choice is always restricted then they are likely to imagine that those books which are not in their ability range are much more attractive than those books which are! Some schools avoid this problem by grading books into broad bands but allowing children to select from a range of bands if they express a preference.

Some schools think that recognising that a book is too difficult is part of learning about book selection and they encourage children to make such judgements. Sometimes children are encouraged to scan the first page of text and to count off a finger of one hand each time they come across a word they do not recognise. If they have used up all five fingers before reaching the end of the page then the book is likely to be very challenging for them.

RECOGNISING THE GENRE OF A BOOK

Children should be aware of the genre of the book they are choosing. Adult reading habits divide distinctly along genre lines with some people choosing to read an almost exclusive diet of science fiction books and others finding their interest lies in romantic fiction. Whilst the National Curriculum specifies the importance of reading from a range of genre, we also need to recognise the development of individual preferences.

Some schools have opted to raise awareness about genre by organising the stock of fiction books in the classroom into genre bands. These can be labelled as such so that all readers are aware of the bands. Of course, some books will straddle two genre divisions and some sensible compromise needs to be reached. It is advisable to involve children in the process of dividing the books into the different genre as the discussion which ensues can be very valuable.

Although we might recognise that ultimate reading pleasures as adults may be from within only one or two genre, it is important that children are given constant opportunities to explore a range of genre. One way to keep a check on children's

READING CHART

Name: _____

Book Title	Author	Date	Modern realistic	Animal	Science fiction	Historical	Mystery	Myths & Legends	Humour	Classic	Stories from different cultures

reading habits is to devise a chart of books (such as the example opposite) which the child has read and which are listed under the heading of the relevant genre. This shows at a glance where the child's preferences lie and which genre they are choosing not to read. It is then possible to discuss why the child should select from a particular genre to keep a balanced reading programme. In order to make helpful suggestions to children about titles of books under the genre they have not previously chosen, it is worth asking other children to share their book charts and for peers to advise on suitable and popular titles. Alternatively, we can ensure that the child's next experience of group reading encompasses a book from the particular genre. Many children can come to enjoy books having first experienced the genre in the support of the group situation.

A chart of reading experiences also shows at a glance exactly what an individual child is reading over the course of a term. This can be very important as it is all too easy to assume that children who choose books regularly and who spend USSR times reading quietly are reading appropriately. Many children use the time exclusively for such 'easy' reading as comic strip books and picture books. Whilst it is important that children have the opportunity to read leisurely, if they get out of the habit of expecting reading to be challenging they are inclined to give up at the first hurdle when obliged to read something more difficult. Of course, books read aloud to children and group reading sessions will help the child to discover the pleasures of texts that make demands of readers, but some of this experience should also be found in private reading.

BOOK SHARING SESSIONS

It is often the practice in the Junior years that children write Book Reviews after they have read a book. The purpose of the review is for the child to reflect upon what they have read and to make some evaluative comments. Some schools give children a framework within which they write their review and this helps to structure their responses. Many children, however, dislike completing book reviews and while it might be useful for a teacher to keep tabs on a child's reading diet, it can discourage children from enjoying their reading knowing that it will end in a written book review. If we consider our reading habits as adults we often return books to the library having thoroughly enjoyed them but we would be very indignant if the librarian suggested that, as a measure of our enjoyment, we wrote a book review! When we have read a good book what we usually want to do is to talk about it and perhaps to persuade other people to read it. Too often the book review is written by a child and read only by the teacher thereby denying the child the opportunity of writing for an audience of peers who might be persuaded by the review to read the book. Children can be encouraged to reflect upon their private reading in 'book share' sessions. These sessions, which could take place weekly, are the opportunity for children to share with others the pleasures (or even disappointments) that they have experienced in their reading. Like a book review, such sessions will be more successful if they have a measure of structure. This can take the form of certain types of headings that the children should cover when discussing the book. There can also be some guidance on the kind of questions that the listeners in the group might pose. These questions can direct children's attention to such things as:

✦ aspects of story structure: plot, characters, complication, resolution etc.;

✦ features of the genre;

✦ similarities with other books.

An example of a prompt sheet for book share sessions appears opposite.

SUMMARY

Opportunities for enjoying fiction need to be extensive and imaginative if children who have developed fluency are also going to develop stamina and commitment. We cannot assume that in undirected private reading children are necessarily going

PROMPT SHEET FOR BOOK SHARE SESSIONS

I have just read ....

by ....

Other titles by .... include

....

This book is about..

....

It is set in ....

The character I liked most is...................................

The character I liked least is ....

The plot hinges on ....

....

....

The best bit in the book is ....

....

....

The dullest bit in the book is ....

....

....

This is a good book for you if ....

....

....

to meet and cope with all the reading requirements specified in the National Curriculum. As teachers we would never consider that children's mathematical ability would develop satisfactorily if, after they had acquired the basic mechanics of computation, they were left to browse with maths books for the remainder of their Junior years. Reading needs to be taught comprehensively if we are to achieve those committed readers Wolfgang Iser describes as 'lost in a book'.

BOOKS SUITABLE FOR READING ALOUD – YEAR 3/YEAR 4

The Frog Prince, Kaye Umansky (1991) Puffin
The Merrythought, Dick King-Smith (1994) Puffin
The Jenius, Dick King-Smith (1994) Gollancz
Taking the Cat's Way Home, Jan Mark (1994) Walker
A Necklace of Raindrops, Joan Aiken (1995) Puffin
Julian, Secret Agent, Ann Cameron (1991) Yearling
The Strawberry Jam Pony, Sheila Lavelle (1989) Young Puffin
Tales of Olga da Polga, Michael Bond (1971) Puffin
The Shrinking of Treehorn, Florence Parry Heide (1984) Young Puffin
It Shouldn't Happen to a Frog, Catherine Storr (1987) Piccolo
Stone Mouse, Jenny Nimmo (1994) Walker
The Enchanted Horse, Magdalen Nabb (1993) Young Lions
Green Monster Magic, Majorie Newman (1990) Young Corgi
Naughtiest Stories, Barbara Ireson (1994) Red Fox
Sink or Swim, Ghillian Potts (1990) Young Corgi
The King of the Copper Mountain, Paul Biegel, Lion Books
Danny Fox, David Thomson (1971) Young Puffin
The Real Thief, William Steit (1989) Farrar, Strause & Giroux
Speccy Four Eyes, Carole Lloyd (1993) Red Fox
Karlo's Tale, Robert Leeson (1993) Young Lions
Ten in a Bed, Allan Ahlberg (1990) Puffin
Stories from Firefly Island, Benedict Blathwayt (1994) Red Fox
Jazeera's Journey, Lisa Bruce (1995) Mammoth
Hazel the Guinea-pig, A. N. Wilson (1990) Walker

Chocolate Porridge, Margaret Mahy (1989) Puffin
Storm, Kevin Crossley-Holland (1985) Heinemann
Mouldy's Orphan, Gillian Avery (1981) Young Puffin
Charlotte's Web, E. B. White (1993) Puffin
Penguin's Progress, Jill Tomlinson (1992) Methuen
The True Story of the Three Little Pigs, Jon Scieszka and Lane Smith (1991) Puffin

BOOKS SUITABLE FOR READING ALOUD –
YEAR 5/YEAR 6

A Taste of Blackberries, Dorish Buchanan Smith (1987) Puffin
The Wrestling Princess, Judy Corbalis (1987) Knight
I, Houdini, Lynne Reid Banks (1989) Lions
The Conjurors Game, Catherine Fisher (1991) Red Fox
Nothing to be Afraid of, Jan Mark (1982) Puffin
The Echoing Green, Mary Rayner (1994) Puffin
A House Inside Out, Penelope Lively (1989) Puffin
Still Waters, Pratima Mitchell (1994) Red Fox
On My Honour, Marion Dane Bauer, (Puffin) (Whittaker 1989)
Underground to Canada, Barbara Smucker (1978) Puffin
Jim Henson's Storyteller, Anthony Minghella (1993) Boxtree
Goodnight Mr Tom, Michelle Magorian (1996) Puffin
Tuck Everlasting, Natalie Babbitt (1988) Farrar, Straus & Giroux
Tales of Splendour, Madhur Jeffrey (1995) Puffin
Squib, Nina Bawden (1973) Puffin
The Village by the Sea, Anita Desai (1992) Puffin
Bill's New Frock, Anne Fine (1994) Mammoth
Martin's Mice, Dick King-Smith (1989) Puffin
Mama's Going to Buy you a Mocking Bird, Jean Little (1986) Puffin
A Pack of Lies, Geraldine McCaughrean (1995) Puffin
The Changeover, Margaret Mahy (1995) Puffin
The Stove Haunting, Bel Mooney (1988) Penguin
The Snow Spider, Jenny Nimmo (1990) Mammoth
The Runaways, Ruth Thomas (1994) Red Fox

Friend or Foe, Michael Morpurgo (1992) Mammoth
The Midnight Fox, Betsy Byars (1976) Puffin
The Mouse and His Child, Russell Hoban (1993) Puffin
Blabber Mouth, Morris Gleitzman (1994) Piper
Mightier Than the Sword, Clare Bevan (1991) Puffin
The Battle of Bubble and Squeak, Phillipa Pearce (1980) Puffin
The Granny Project, Anne Fine (1990) Mammoth
How Green You Are! Berlie Doherty (1992) Mammoth
The Way to Sattin Shore, Philippa Pearce (1985) Puffin
The Exiles, Hilary McKay (1993) Lions
Hideaway, Ruth Thomas (1995) Red Fox
Princess Jazz and the Angels, Rachel Anderson (1995) Mammouth

REFERENCES

Barthes, R. (1985) 'Day by day with Roland Barthes', from Blonsky, M. (Ed.) *On Signs*, John Hopkins University Press.
Beard, R. (1990) *Developing Reading 3–13*, Hodder & Stoughton.
Bell, N. (1989) 'Visualising and verbalizing for language comprehension', American Imagery Conference.
Chambers, A. (1991) *The Reading Environment*, The Thimble Press.
Chambers, A. (1993) *Tell Me: Children, Reading and Talk*, The Thimble Press.
Fine, A. (1996) *Flour Babies*, Penguin.
Hook, J. and Lutrario, C. (1994) *Hooked on Books*, Collins Educational.
Howe, J. (1994) *The Celery Stalks at Midnight*, Piper.
Iser, W. (1978) *The Act of Reading*, John Hopkins University Press.
Kastner, E. (1995) *Emil and the Detectives*, Red Fox.
Kemp, G. (1994) *The Turbulent Term of Tyke Tiler*, Puffin.
Martin, T. and Leather, B. (1994) *Readers and Texts in the Primary Years*, Open University Press.
Pullman, P. (1994) *The Ruby in the Smoke*, Puffin.

Rosenblatt, L. (1978) *The Reader, the Text and the Poem*, Southern Illinois University Press.

Tolkien, J. R. (1995) *The Hobbit*, HarperCollins.

Tomlinson, J. (1992) *The Owl Who was Afraid of the Dark*, Mammoth.

Wilson, J. (1992) *The Story of Tracy Beaker*, Yearling.

English in the National Curriculum (1995), HMSO.

The Bullock Report (1977), HMSO.

CHAPTER 2

DEVELOPING THE READING OF NON-FICTION

Different demands are made upon readers of fiction and non-fiction; this chapter suggests ways to help young readers (8 to 12 years) adopt an appropriate way of reading non-fiction texts. It also looks at the different genre and their characteristics. Some basic considerations are offered to help teachers to make a more informed choice when selecting non-fiction books. Practical ideas and activities are suggested and linked to the appropriate skill.

> Children should read from a wide range of sources of information, including those not specifically designed for children... Pupils should be taught how to find information in books and computer based sources by using organisational devices to help them decide which parts of the material to read closely. They should be given opportunities to read for different purposes, adopting appropriate strategies for the task, including skimming to gain an overall impression, scanning to locate information and detailed reading to obtain specific information.
>
> National Curriculum KS2 Reading 1. Range (a), HMSO 1995.

THE IMPORTANCE OF LEARNING TO READ NON-FICTION

In the course of their life, even the most ardent reader of fiction is likely to spend far more time reading the myriad of non-fiction materials than narrative. Traditionally it was presumed that if children could read fiction easily then they should not experience any problems reading non-fiction. Since the research undertaken in the 1970s (E Lunzer and K Gardner, *The Effective Use of Reading* (1979) Heinemann), however, there has been a growing awareness that proficiency in one form of reading does not necessarily mean mastery over another. It is now recognised that reading of fiction and non-fiction require very different approaches and children need to be taught the skills involved in reading non-fiction as carefully as they are taught how to read fiction. Children are generally taught to read from fiction and much of their language experience in Key Stage 1 will have involved listening and responding to stories. Although much more non-fiction is being introduced into these classrooms it is still the case that when children read for themselves they are far more confident with reading stories than non-fiction.

> Fiction, marvellous as it is as an art form, is a poor training for the reading of non-narrative. The story carries the reader along and stimulates the understanding of a text without too much conscious effort. When those pupil readers hit a text explaining facts or arguments they expect the same thing to work and are disappointed and baffled when it does not.
>
> Marland, M. *Education Guardian* (13/11/90)

THE DIFFERENCE BETWEEN FICTION AND NON-FICTION TEXTS

In order for teachers to help children to become confident readers of non-fiction texts we need to be aware of the different demands that non-fiction makes upon the reader and to show children how to read these texts.

DIFFERENCES BETWEEN TEXTS

Fiction

Is generally read from beginning to end, using a fast fluent read
Is generally written in the past tense
Has a plot and story-line
Relates events to each other so that the reader can predict

what may happen

Needs very little teacher introduction, there is no need to know about the characters or plot

Is illustrated by pictures

Dates very slowly

Uses a high proportion of personal pronouns

There is no need to consult other books

Is presented in a similar format (chapters)

The meaning of unknown vocabulary can often be gleaned from the rest of the text

There is no need for the reader to question the validity of the text

The author generally tries to build up a relationship with the reader, the style is friendly and attractive

Non-fiction

Needs a broken, selected, reflective read

Is generally written in the present tense

The contents and order are generally the choice of the author

Is unlikely to have a defined order

The teacher needs to establish readers' knowledge and to give a specific aim for extracting further knowledge

Is illustrated by charts, maps, photographs, diagrams, pictures

Dates very quickly

Uses a high proportion of impersonal pronouns

It is often necessary to use a variety of subject related books

Contains a wide variety of forms (index, glossary, contents, notes, bibliography)

Uses specific terms which need to be understood

The reader needs to check the accuracy of the text

Texts often seek to preserve the anonymity of the author. Authorial voice is distant and reserved

CONTINUOUS READING VS. INTERRUPTED READ

Research undertaken by Lunzer and Gardner (1979) showed that children expected to read non-fiction in the same way as they read fiction. Children generally learn to read from stories and hear far more fiction texts read aloud by the teacher. They associate reading with a continuous story-line, read with fluency and expression so, when they are presented with non-fiction they apply the same reading approach. In fact when we read non-fiction it requires a broken and reflective read. We read a few sentences and then mentally check the information to see if it increases our knowledge or confirms what we already know. We need both to demonstrate and explain how to read non-fiction texts to children. If the new information is considerable we generally make notes or jot down headings to remind us of the content. This is rarely necessary when we hear a story as its logical form helps us to remember the events. Too often children think that they are expected to remember every fact; they do not separate the facts they already knew from those they have just read. In desperation they copy out the paragraph or page hoping that this will cover every requirement.

EVERYDAY LANGUAGE VS. FORMAL LANGUAGE

Non-fiction is often written in the impersonal passive voice. It rarely contains spoken language and children find that this distance from everyday language makes the texts seem too weighty and difficult to penetrate. Consider this sentence: 'Where the desert met the cultivated land of the valley, the Valley Temple was built.' If we were telling someone about this or writing the information in a story it is much more likely that we would start with the subject of the sentence, and then provide some details rather than the other way round.

If we want children to learn how to read non-fiction texts then we must make non-fiction a part of our reading aloud sessions. We need to read and then stop to talk about what the author is saying. Encourage the children to raise questions about parts that they either did not understand or want to know more about.

LINKED INFORMATION VS. MORE ARBITRARY ORDER

Fiction texts are organic: each item of information relates to another item. The reader can, therefore, make predictions so the text seems to flow freely as the reader continually anticipates the next part of the story. Fiction readers are expected to recall generalisations and to make personal responses to the story.

Non-fiction texts are not organic: each item of information is self- sufficient and the order in which facts are presented is, to a large extent, arbitrary. The non-fiction reader is expected to retain specific information but not to make personal responses when reading information. It is difficult to make predictions about non-fiction and it is making predictions that weaves the reader into the text. It becomes a creative act. Non-fiction can leave the reader on the outside as a passive observer.

When children read non-fiction they need to:
• recognise the kind of text they are reading
• know what they are expected to recall after reading the text
• understand what they will be expected to do with that information.   Unless they are shown how to read, how to access the information and have a clear idea about what they should do with the information, we will not put them in control of these texts.

THE GENRE OF NON-FICTION

As we have become more aware of the distinctive features of texts, theorists have started to argue that these features place a text with a certain 'genre'. Books may be divided into two main genre – fiction and non-fiction – and further sub-divided into more specific genre. Within the genre of fiction, for example, we might describe a book as a mystery, romance, detective, science-fiction or historical novel, etc. Many non-fiction books contain more than one form of writing so we need to understand the salient features of the writing form in order to communicate our own ideas.

The main types of non-fiction genre are widely agreed to be:

Recount   A story-like genre – diaries, journals

Report   Factual information is given but not explained – atlases, dictionaries, maps, diagrams

Procedure   Instructions for an activity – instructions, directions, rules, recipes

Explanation Explaining why something happened – natural or social process of how something works

Exposition   Persuasion – advertising, brochures, argument

Discussion   Presenting different points of view – reports containing recommendations.

Children who recognise which genre they are reading, and when the author has changed to a different genre (for example from report to exposition), are more likely to read with understanding and to bring a critical eye to the writing. We need to draw children's attention to the features of these genre and help them to become confident readers and writers of these genres.

TEXT LAYOUT AND LANGUAGE STRUCTURE OF THE DIFFERENT NON-FICTION GENRE

RECOUNT

This genre is used to retell events, usually from a personal point of view. It is used mostly in diaries and journals. The text is generally written in the past tense and presented in a chronological order.

	Saturday 20th June 1942	*written in*
	I haven't written for a few days, because I <u>wanted</u> first	*past tense*
	of all to think about my diary. It's an odd idea for	
text	someone like me to keep a diary; not only because <u>I</u>	*written in*
written in a	have never done so before, but because it seems to me	*1st person*
chronological	that neither I – nor for that matter anyone else – will	
order	be interested in the unbosomings of a thirteen year old	
	schoolgirl. <u>Still what does it matter? I want to write</u>,	*contains*
	but more than that I want to bring out all kinds of	*personal*
	things that lie buried deep in my heart.	*reflection*
	The Diary of Anne Frank	

REPORT

This genre is used to describe the way things are, including both natural phenomena and social structures. This style of writing is generally used for textbooks, and uses the present tense (unless referring to something that is now extinct) and there is no temporal sequence. The text usually starts with a general statement followed by a description of the appearance or habits of the subject.

general opening statement	The Slug — *use of present tense*
	Slugs are unusual creatures because they have no male or female slugs – all slugs <u>are</u> both male and female, they both have eggs and sperm. So any slug can mate
author choice of order of statements	with any other slug of the same species.——————— *no personal comment*
	In the spring and early summer the slugs mate and lay their eggs in damp places in the earth. *use of short sentences*
	<u>It usually takes about a month for the eggs to hatch.</u> The young slug looks like the adult but it is smaller and often lighter in colour.

each paragraph usually contains one fact

PROCEDURE

This genre describes how something is accomplished through a series of actions or sequenced steps. It is more about the process rather than being an explanation about why something occurs. There is often a specific chronological order to the text, for example in a recipe or in the rules for a game, and the command form (or imperative) of the verb is used.

list of ingredients	Making an omelette
	Ingredients: 2 eggs knob of butter
	salt and pepper *instructions given in short statements*
ellipsis of 'you' and use of simple present tense	<u>Break</u> the eggs into a dish.
	<u>Add</u> the salt and pepper and whisk lightly.
	<u>Melt</u> the butter into a pan and, when hot, add the beaten eggs. *no explanation given*
chronological order	When the omelette <u>begins to set</u> draw the edges of the omelette gently towards the middle.
	When the top of the omelette is set fold it in half and put it onto a warm plate.

EXPLANATION

This genre aims to explain the processes involved in natural and social phenomena. It is generally concerned with non-human topics, for example the stages of a butterfly, the rain cycle, how a car engine works.

	Where does rain come from?	*title often given as a question*
opening statement giving little explanation	Most of the water we use comes from the rain that falls from the sky. The rain collects in puddles, lakes, ponds and streams. Small streams join up to make large rivers which flow into the sea. When it stops raining, the puddles seem to disappear.	*use of 'because' and 'then'*
detailed explanation given	The water disappears <u>because</u> the heat of the sun turns the water into water vapour. This is very difficult to see. <u>Then</u> the vapour <u>rises up</u> into the sky.	*written in present tense*
	This is called <u>evaporation.</u> *use of specific terms*	

EXPOSITION

This genre generally puts forward one point of view or argument, for the purpose of persuasion, for example an advertisement, a letter of complaint, an article about racism. The text usually starts with an opening statement and develops an argument but only states one point of view.

	School Uniform	
opening statement states point of view	There is no doubt that school uniform is both valuable and sensible. The clothes are designed to ensure comfort and ease of movement. The colours are carefully chosen so that the dirt does not show.	*focus on generic rather than specific*
states reasons and builds up argument	<u>Another reason</u> that is given is that it ensures that all children look the same and do not compete with each other over brand names causing endless expense to their parents. <u>Moreover</u> the child's school is	*uses present tense*
uses logical relation words	easily recognised by the uniform and consequently <u>should</u> any poor behaviour on public transport or in the street be observed it can be reported to the school.	*often uses modality: could, should, might*

DISCUSSION

Texts in this genre present information about and arguments for both sides of an issue. Conclusions generally support the point of view of the writer but both sides of the argument have been considered.

	Should we have Zoos in this country?	use of present tense
states the debate and offers two points of view	The current debate over the question of whether to retain the zoos we have in this country or gradually to close them down <u>continues</u> to rage. As <u>we have</u> become more aware of the environment and the vital place that animals and plants play in maintaining a balance in nature, so the subject of whether we should have zoos which contain animals from very different habitats has arisen.	often uses personal pronouns
arguments are put forward with supporting statements	It is recognised that zoos have saved many animals from extinction <u>but</u> as the countries of world becomes more aware of the danger of extinction to their specific species, so it seems unnecessary to transport endangered animals to a different environment, <u>rather</u> than giving them extra protection in their own habitat. Zoos do allow people to see animals they might otherwise never see but travel round the world is much easier today and the extensive coverage on television of rare animals does give people a very good picture of these animals.	sentences contain both points of view use of causal connectives eg. rather, therefore, because
concludes with the writer taking a side in the argument	In conclusion it is obvious that both points of view can put forward strong arguments. Nevertheless, <u>I would</u> support those experts who believe that we should try to protect animals in their own environments.	uses writer's own voice in conclusion

If children are taught to recognise the characteristics of these various different genre, they can begin to anticipate what the text is trying to do and to evaluate how far it achieves its purpose. They become aware of the significance of important features of the text, for example, the appropriateness of the language used for its purpose, content and audience. When readers have mastery over a text and its form they have a better understanding of the text, the nature of the message it contains and how this information should be interpreted.

In reflecting upon the form of the writing, children may also begin to understand how *they* should write when asked to write in a specific genre.

The different graphs used to show comparison (similarity and difference) are: bar chart, pie chart, line graph and pictogram.

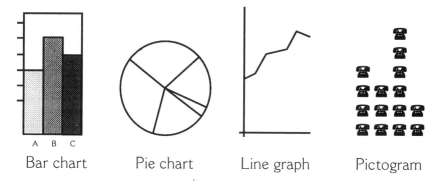

| Bar chart | Pie chart | Line graph | Pictogram |

The following diagrams are used to help with classification: tree diagram, Venn diagram, topic web and attributes matrix.

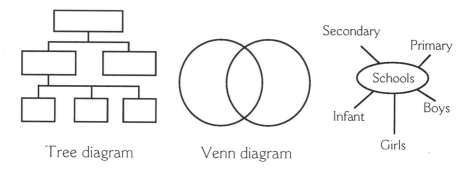

Tree diagram   Venn diagram

The following illustrations show where things are positioned: map, distribution network and scale drawing plan.

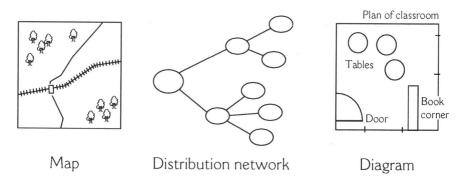

Map   Distribution network   Diagram

The following illustrations are used to show when things will happen or have happened: time-line and flow diagram.

Register	Break	Lunch	Art	Home
9.00 a.m.	11.00 a.m.	12.30 p.m.	2.00 p.m.	3.00 p.m.

Time-line

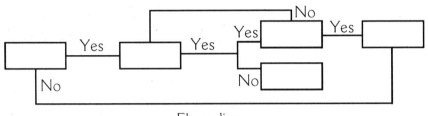

Flow diagram

ACTION

1. Use a 'big book' to show the group these various different graphic aids. Demonstrate how these help to display information so that readers can 'see at a glance' what they need to know. Explain how it is easier to compare things when put into a diagram than when they are written in continuous text. Start by showing the children the uses of the bar graph as this is the easiest for them to understand.

2. Ask the group to find some information to put on to a bar graph. For example, the number of boys that have dark hair or fair hair and the number of girls that have dark hair or fair hair. Display the bar graph on the wall and ask the children to help you to 'read' the information.

3. Devise activities to cover the other graphic aids. For example, the children might draw a Venn diagram on how they get to school. How many come by car? How many sometimes come by car and sometimes walk? How many always walk? They could devise a time-line on their life; a pie chart to divide

up how they spend the time in the classroom; a chart to show in what ways some animals are the same and in what ways they are different; a map to show a stranger how to find their classroom; devise a family tree for a character in a book, for example Red Riding Hood.

READING RATE SKILLS

When we read fiction it is expected that the reader will start at the beginning and read through the text to the last page. When reading non-fiction it is very rare that readers need to read through from the beginning to the end. Rather, they need to skim the text and select sections to scan to see if the information they are seeking is on the page. Children do need to be given opportunities to practise these skills.

ACTION

Scanning:

Provide a sample text for the children and have two specific questions prepared to which they need to find the answer. Demonstrate to the children how you scan down the page, often reading only the first line of a paragraph or seeking out the words in bold. When we are trying to scan quickly we make a decision to omit text that seems unlike to provide the answer. Ask the children to scan down the text to see if they can find the paragraph which is likely to have the answer to your question in it. When they can do this ask them to turn to another page and, working in pairs, devise questions for their classmates. They should then swap texts and try to scan down the page to find the answers as quickly as possible.

Skimming:

Explain to the children that skimming is generally used to locate text which the reader then scans down in order to find the specific information. For example, we skim through the telephone directory looking for the alphabetical page which contains the initial letter of the name, we skim through these pages to isolate the specific page on which the name will occur.

We scan down that page to locate the actual telephone number.

Children need clear and careful teaching of all these locational skills in order to become quick and proficient at finding the information they need. Consequently, they need frequent opportunities to use these skills. Often, the teacher and the child are more concerned to find the facts and the teaching of **how** to find them is overlooked. When sharing non-fiction books with children we constantly need to model how we are using them.

HELPING CHILDREN TO UNDERSTAND HOW TO READ NON-FICTION

Unless we demonstrate and discuss how to read non-fiction, children will apply the same approach to non-fiction that they use with fiction. The most important research that looked at children's reading for learning strategies was undertaken by Lunzer and Gardner (1979). They pointed out that for texts to be fully understood an *interrupted* read is necessary. They advocated that this kind of reading is best carried out in groups where children can stop and talk and question as they read. They highlighted the problem that in real life we only read non-fiction on a topic that interests us and generally because we have a specific need to find the information. In school we assume the *interest* and *invent* the need. If children do not have a genuine purpose for seeking information, however, their study is likely to be perfunctory and they pass the time copying out large chunks of texts straight from the book. Children learn how to tackle an information book by watching and mimicking an effective reader.

Set time aside to read aloud from an information book and demonstrate how you first seek for the information and then use an interrupted read.
• Introduce the book and tell the class why you selected it.
• Ask the class to think of three questions that the book might answer.

• Write the questions down on the board.
• Read the contents page to the children and ask them if any of the chapters sound as if they might provide the answers.
• Ask the children what words they would suggest for reference in the index.
• Show the class how you use the index. Talk about skimming and scanning down the page.
• Decide which chapter (or section) you are going to read aloud. Talk about its location and layout. Is there any part which looks more useful than another?
• Read with intonation and expression, stop and reread those sentences that you think are of special interest. Comment as you read and, if appropriate, look in the glossary.
• After reading ask the children to tell you about any piece of information that is new to them.
• Ask them to tell you anything that has helped them to answer the questions written on the board.
• Ask whether this has raised new questions and, if so, what would they do to find out the answers to these?
• Talk about the language of the section you have read. Point out words that are specific to the genre of the passage. Encourage them to use these words when talking about the information. For example, 'however', 'on the other hand', 'therefore' and 'as a result'.

CHOOSING NON-FICTION

When choosing non-fiction books for the classroom the following considerations should be taken into account:
• What is the date of the publication? Information books can become dated very easily and unless it specifies that it is a new edition it is necessary to check that the information is up-to-date. Think how much the map of Europe has changed over the last five years!
• How is the information in the book organised? Is the contents page informative? Does the index seem clear and accessible?

- Is the overall organisation good? Are there clear headings and side-headings? How does the book use bold? Is there a useful glossary or are the definitions written using a vocabulary that is more difficult than the original word?
- To what extent is the text illustrated by diagrams and photographs? Are these decorative or informative?
- How difficult is the language? Are the sentences written clearly and simply? Is the terminology explained in the text or referenced to a glossary?
- Would the book make a useful reference in the school library? Does it fill a gap in your library?

> A schools collection of non-fiction should include both 'bread and butter' books and a good selection of lively, thought-provoking books to encourage voluntary reading and browsing. Mallet (1994)

DISPLAYING NON-FICTION BOOKS IN THE CLASSROOM

Wray and Lewis (1992) pointed out the need to organise books in the classroom carefully. Their research showed that where there was a clear system of organisation which had been explained to the children, much better use was made of the books. They also found, however, that there was little consistency between classes and they pointed out that this was essential if children were to remain confident users of non-fiction texts.

A FRAMEWORK FOR ENCOURAGING CHILDREN TO READ AND RESPOND TO NON-FICTION

PREPARATION FOR READING

Before introducing the books, brainstorm with the children what they already know about the subject and find out what they would like to know. This focuses their attention on the subject and gives the teacher knowledge about their level of understanding and the vocabulary they have already learnt.

Ask the children to work in pairs or groups and to write down brief notes on anything they already know about the subject. Let them write this on to a 'What I know about...' chart. Ask them to devise two questions on the topic. Share this knowledge with the class or group.

FOCUSING ON TEXTS

Let the children find relevant books on the topic or provide a variety of textbooks. Show them how to skim through the books and ensure they know how to use the locational aids.

Action: Ask the children to discuss the information they can find out from the cover and the blurb. Devise a set of true or false questions that require the children to skim and scan through the book for the information. Working in pairs, ask the children to set ten questions that can be answered by using the contents and index. Let them swap the question sheets with another pair to see if they can find the answers. Finally, return the original questions to the children who first set them to be marked.

RESEARCHING

The most important reading activity occurs when the children are asked to research the topic using the books. To do this they will need to skim, scan and practise the interrupted read. They will have to make decisions about the content of a passage and its relevance. They may have to consult the glossary. They will need to make notes and reference pages that they might need for future activities.

Action: Decide which children should research specific aspects of a topic and explain that they will be the expert on that particular information. Tell them to start by making a list of the relevant sections of the books that they think will be useful. Select a short topic or 2-4 pages or a double page spread and tell the children to make notes about the subject. When they have completed their notes, give them questions to answer. They should try to answer these questions from their notes and not from the reference text. Finally, they should check their answers by referring to the original text. Remember that trying to write something in 'your own words' is incredibly difficult if an expert has already written it. (Even adults copy texts but they call it 'Quotations'.) So, to prevent mindless copying of chunks of material, ensure that the children have to present the data in a different form from the one they have read. For example, they might make a chart, poster, brochure, list or quiz for their classmates.

PRESENTING THE INFORMATION

Most children want to share new knowledge and, if they have been put into the position of being an expert, then they need to present this to an audience. If the whole class has undertaken the same activity there is little incentive to talk about the learning or to demonstrate what they know.

Action: Let the group decide how they wish to present the information. This could be as a quiz, chart, '20 questions', documentary, writing a magazine article for display on the classroom wall, wanted poster, or writing captions and newspaper headlines.

SUMMARY

To ensure that children become proficient and confident readers of non-fiction we have to:
• demonstrate to them *how* to read non-fiction;
• ensure that they become familiar with the conventions of non-fiction books;
• provide them with reasons to read and retain the information.
  They have to become competent in understanding information books if they are to become independent readers who can cope with the demands of Key Stage Three. Teaching the skills of reading non-fiction as well as showing children the purpose of reading information is, therefore, vital.

REFERENCES

Lewis, M. and Wray, D. (1995) *Developing Children's Non-fiction Writing*, Scholastic Ltd.

Littlefair, A. (1991) *Reading all Kinds of Writing*, Open University Press.

Lunzer, E. and Gardner, K. (Eds.) (1979) *The Effective Use of Reading*, Heinemann.

Mallet, M. (1994) *Reading Non-fiction in the Primary Years: A Language and Learning Approach*, NATE.

Wray, D. and Lewis, M. (1992) 'Primary children's use of information books', from *Reading November 1992*, UKRA.

FURTHER READING

Littlefair, A. (1992) *Genres in the Classroom* Minibook 1, UKRA.

Mallet, M. (1992) *Making Facts Matter: Reading Non-fiction 5–11*, Paul Chapman.

Neate, B. (1993) *Finding Out About Finding Out: A Practical Guide to Children's Information Books*, Hodder & Stoughton.

Von Schweinitz, E. (March 1989) 'Facing the facts' from *Books for Keeps*.

CHAPTER 3

DEVELOPING THE READING OF POETRY

Children's language skills can flourish within the context of thoroughly enjoyable poetry. Very young children have a natural inclination towards rhythm, rhyme, word play and repetition. Their enthusiasm is nurtured by early years teachers who provide in their classrooms a rich poetic culture of songs, poems, nursery rhymes and action games. Nevertheless, as children grow older their resistance to poetry tends to increase, culminating in an adult culture which is almost starved of poetry. This chapter looks at the reasons for this change in attitude and offers practical suggestions to prevent it taking place. If reading and writing poetry, talking about poetry and listening to poetry are pleasurable and regular activities for primary school children, then not only will their language skills develop but they will have acquired the key to a richly expressive medium.

OVERCOMING RESISTANCE TO POETRY

Many older children do not like poetry. A large proportion of adults in our society regard poetry with suspicion, fear and, in some cases, loathing. Even teachers can be sometimes heard to confess that they are not great fans of poetry outside of school. It is as if these feelings are passed on to children as they grow older.

These negative feelings may be a consequence of the dry, academic poetry lessons of our own school days. Enjoyment and pleasure hardly came into the equation for many secondary learners in the past. Lessons were composed of the dissection and analysis of a limited selection of difficult historical poems. Our perceptions of poetry now may still be so narrow that we keep poetry at a distance, associating it with past discomfort and boredom. With this background, resistance to poetry is understandable.

Nowadays, however, resistance is less appropriate. The range of poetry available to Junior children is exciting; teaching methods are more creative and enjoyment matters. We need to dispel the myths about poetry so that we can help children to open up their thinking, challenge their pre-conceived ideas and motivate their poetry reading.

POPULAR MYTHS ABOUT POETRY

MYTH 1 – READING POETRY IS AN ACADEMIC, ELITIST ACTIVITY

Academic study of literature, including poetry, is a worthwhile strand of our cultural and educational systems. It is, however, merely one of many strands.

Just because we do not or cannot engage with the academic strand in our education, career, or in our choices for leisure does not mean that we have failed, or are in some way poetically inferior. Nevertheless, a feeling of inadequacy and consequent low self-esteem relating to poetry turns rapidly into negativity and this is the point, sadly, at which many people reject poetry for the rest of their lives. Such rejection can eliminate opportunities for pleasure, transmission of cultural and multi-cultural traditions and the development and organic growth of new language. The recent surge of 'rapping', for instance, is a wonderful example of the joy of playing creatively with words, and yet very few probably recognise it for what it is - one of the many forms of poetry!

The academic strand should, of course, be accessible as a choice to those who have an interest in such an approach. However, in order to reach a point where everyone has an equal opportunity to make that choice from an informed standpoint, all pupils need to have firm foundations of knowledge, skills, understanding and confidence which can be applied to literature. The nurturing environment provided in the early years of education needs to be continued and developed through meaningful, enjoyable and appropriate activities, through which the pupils can engage with poetic forms and feel a strong sense of ownership, power and control. In this way, those who do not, or cannot follow the academic strand are still able to enjoy and appreciate the poetry in their lives, rather than feeling excluded from such an entitlement.

ACTION → *Prioritise the enjoyment and pleasure of poetry.*

MYTH 2 – POETRY IS DIFFICULT AND BORING

Inappropriate use of poetry which is too complex or too difficult will put children off a task more quickly than lightning! Children cannot be expected to understand and appreciate the use of metaphor and simile if they have never had fun opportunities to play with words themselves. Similarly, the subject matter needs to be meaningful and relevant so that children can relate and respond to what they read. Match the subject matter and terminology with the children's level of ability and it will not be too difficult or boring. Plan progression carefully rather than leaving it to chance (See page 81 on 'Differentiation and progression'.)

ACTION → *Choose materials carefully, according to interest value and ability levels.*

MYTH 3 – POETRY HAS TO RHYME

Most teachers will recall reading contrived and inappropriate vocabulary which children have forced into their poems to make them rhyme. Many poems do not rhyme but children will model their writing on what they know. It is crucial, therefore, that they have examples of many different styles on which to model their own work. Children need opportunities to evaluate the effectiveness of different words within the same rhyme scheme, and sometimes consider whether the rhyme is even necessary at all.

ACTION → *Ensure that you do not just read rhyming poems to the children, and discuss this aspect of form regularly.*

MYTH 4 – POETRY IS OLD AND IRRELEVANT

Children's views on poetry are quite likely to reflect the anthologies on their teacher's shelf. If they are only ever exposed to choices from *The Book of a Thousand Poems*, their perceptions will be influenced by that selection. There are wonderfully colourful and challenging anthologies available to teachers today in addition to collections of poets' works. These include an exciting and growing amount of modern poetry from a range of cultures in addition to collections from the past. (See the list of new and relevant poetry on page 77.)

ACTION → *Ensure that you provide a good balance of stimulating classic and relevant modern poetry which reflect a range of cultures.*

MYTH 5 – POETRY ALWAYS HAS TO BE ANALYSED TO BE APPRECIATED

Analysis is important if children are to develop a critical awareness of what they read. Opportunities should be available to share and discuss responses to poetry. These opportunities need to be active, stimulating and fruitful occasions rather than arduous and academic ones. (See page 79 for suggestions of suitable activities.) Remember also that there should sometimes be opportunities to read and listen to poetry without taking the poem apart. Responses can be enjoyed, savoured or reflected upon in the moment, before moving on to something else.

ACTION → *Beware of 'discussing to death' every poem you share with the children – sometimes it is enough to say how it makes you feel.*

MYTH 6 – POETRY IS SERIOUS

Children tend to be natural humorists, and respond well to the inclusion of humour within the classroom whatever the context. If they are only ever exposed to poetry of a serious and adult nature, they will become resigned to a fixed notion of poetry. Opening up the world of poetry to children means that we very often have to approach it on their terms. Playing with words for fun can be a rich place for concept building, and humorous poetry, rhymes and rap can attract children to read poetry from choice.

This does not mean that serious poetry should be excluded from Junior classrooms. Far from it. There is much to be gained from thought-provoking material. However, if the myth is to be dispelled, there must be a good balance of poetry of all types, including humour.

ACTION → *Include jokes, limericks, funny rhymes, rap, etc. in the resources available*

WHY TEACH POETRY?

To teach poetry because the National Curriculum says we must is pragmatic but insufficient. Now that we have overcome resistance to poetry, let us list all the benefits of including it on the primary curriculum.

EXPLORATION OF LANGUAGE FORMS

Listening to and reading poetry allows children to experience and explore the world of language. They can do this with other texts as well, of course, but poetry provides ideal, self-contained units to discuss, evaluate and compare. It also provides an extremely broad range of language forms to enjoy. Children can explore:

the structural form or design framework

◆ use of verse pattern
◆ rhyme and rhythm
◆ syllable poems such as Haiku
◆ fixed forms such as limericks and sonnets
◆ free form such as shape poems and descriptive narrative.

the use of figurative language

◆ simile and metaphor
◆ alliteration
◆ onomatopoeia
◆ word economy
◆ puns.

These aspects of figurative language might be regarded as the building materials used within the framework. Another analogy to describe the relationship between these two parts might be that of a painting, where the 'structure' is the shape of the picture pattern, and the 'figurative form' is the use of colour and texture.

UNDERSTANDING NEW PERSPECTIVES

Listening to and reading poetry can provide children with a challenging range of points of view. Poems are distinctly personal to the poets who write them. They describe and narrate in quite individual ways – ways which represent very personal views and emotions about all manner of subjects and which demonstrate the diversity of human perception. Children who are engaged in a topic on World War Two, for example, cannot fail to be stimulated and challenged by the range of war poetry. Some poets have written about glory and patriotism, whilst others have focused on the waste of human life, such as Anne Harvey's 'In Time of War' (1987), Blackie.

RESPONSES TO AN ART FORM

When a poet writes a poem, he or she is creating a piece of art. Raw materials (ideas and words) are being shaped into a structure which can be experienced by others. Others may react in a range of emotions and opinions. This brings us into the world of response, which is central to the reading of poetry. There may, of course, be occasions when we read a poem for information, war poems for example, include much historical evidence, but it is more usual that the poem is read for a response. As we encourage Junior readers towards more sophisticated modes of response, poetry provides an excellent resource for this purpose.

TRANSMISSION OF CULTURAL TRADITIONS

To say that we read poetry to support the cultural heritage of English Literature is outmoded in present-day British society. Of course, there is no denying that the heritage of English Literature should have a place in our poetry curriculum, but today it is one of several important aspects of cultural transmission. It may be that the acknowledgement of this broadening of cultures and traditions will encourage more people to feel a real ownership of poetry as it reflects their lives. The mill songs of late nineteenth century working class

Lancashire weavers have just as much right to an audience as the poems of Keats. The vibrant rhythms of Caribbean poets can enrich our lives with their colourful sounds and images. Sad reflections on the pollution of the environment are as vital as lyrical descriptions of daffodils on mossy banks.

Eawr Johnny

Eawr Johnny's started coartin'
'E's asked 'er reawnd for tea.
Ah corn't 'elp wonderin' what
'er's like –
It's 'is very fust girl, dost see.
'Is Dad's talked to 'im, man to
man,
Grandad's been givin' advice.
Ah just said, "Behave yersel'"
An' noticed 'e looked nice.
'E took care when 'e dressed
'iself –
'E even washed 'is neck.
'E's tidied up 'is bedroom –
It's usually a wreck.
'E says 'e'll marry Susan –
Ah couldn't 'elp but smile.
In mi mind's eye, Ah saw 'em
both
Walking deawnt' church aisle.
So Grandad's put 'is teeth in
An' promised not to swear.
'Is Dad's got 'is best white shirt
on
An' Ah've specially set mi 'air.
Tea's aw ready waitin'
Everything looks fine.
There's jelly, cakes an' ice-cream –
Just right, for the age o' nine.

Nellie Crutchlow
Just Sithabod

Chicken Dinner

Mama, don' do it, please,
Don' cook dat chicken fe dinner,
We know dat chicken from she hatch,
She is de only one in de batch
Dat de mongoose didn' catch,
Please don' cook her fe dinner.

Mama, don' do it, please,
Don' cook dat chicken fe dinner,
Yuh mean to tell mi yuh feget
Yuh promise her to we as a pet
She not even have a chance to lay yet
An yuh want to cook her fe dinner.

Mama, don' do it, please,
Don' cook dat chicken fe dinner,
Don' give Henrietta de chop,
Ah tell yuh what, we could swop,
We will get yuh one from de shop,
If yuh promise not to cook her fe dinner.

Mama, me really glad, yuh know,
Yuh never cook Henny fe dinner,
An she glad too, ah bet,
Oh Lawd, me suddenly feel upset,
Yuh don' suppose is somebody else pet
We eating now fe dinner?
A Caribbean Dozen

The Kitten at Play

See the kitten on the wall,
Sporting with the leaves that fall,
Withered leaves, one, two and three,
Falling from the elder-tree;

Through the calm and frosty air
Of the morning bright and fair.

See the kitten, how she starts,
Crouches, stretches, paws and darts;
With a tiger-leap half way
Now she meets her coming prey.
Lets it go as fast as then
Has it in her power again.

Now she works with three and four,
Like an Indian conjurer;
Quick as he in feats of art,
Gracefully she plays her part;
Yet were gazing thousands there,
What would little Tabby care?
William Wordsworth
The Book of a Thousand Poems

Historical literary treasures from England, Ireland, Scotland and Wales remain an important feature of the poetry curriculum. There has been a growth in English interest in Celtic culture which is reflected in popular music, artefacts and books. There is also much to be learned from examining the historical changes in the form of language and vocabulary. The requirements to teach standard English and grammar can be greatly supported by the use of such material; learning about former rules helps us to understand the rules of today. Breaking the old rules of poetry has been a significant feature of certain periods of literary history, knowing this helps to understand the present day modes. We need to know and understand the rules of form if we are to creatively break them!

Breaks with tradition become part of a new tradition. Old traditions are put in a new context. Our multi-cultural society is an example of a change in our concept of heritage and cultural transmission. This change has brought us new riches in terms of literature and language; the range of poetry available now is more diverse and fascinating than ever before.

DEVELOPING KNOWLEDGE, SKILLS AND UNDERSTANDING

The following check-lists provide a guide to the main elements which might be explored with children at different stages of their Junior years. It must be recognised that a well-planned and developmental approach will enhance the teaching of these elements. The skill being taught must be matched to the children's level of ability. It is far better to engage children's interest in using adverbs and adjectives confidently in early Junior years and then to introduce the labels in more challenging identification of the parts of speech later on. (Sequencing and progression are discussed in more detail on page 80.)

KNOWLEDGE

- ✦ vowel and consonant
- ✦ extended vocabulary
- ✦ adverbs, adjectives, conjunctions, pronouns
- ✦ verb tenses
- ✦ rhythm
- ✦ syllable
- ✦ simile – one thing likened to another
- ✦ metaphor – one thing described in terms of another
- ✦ onomatopoeia – indicates the meaning by its sound
- ✦ alliteration – repetition of initial consonant sounds
- ✦ image – pictures we conjure in our imagination
- ✦ stanza – correct name for a verse
- ✦ rhyme scheme – arrangement of the rhymes in a poem
- ✦ parody – imitating the work of another poet for fun
- ✦ narrative – telling a story or relating events
- ✦ variety of form and presentation

SKILLS

- ✦ reading poetry alone
- ✦ reading aloud with expression
- ✦ expressing a response
- ✦ retelling
- ✦ organising ideas
- ✦ relating to own experience
- ✦ planning alternative sections
- ✦ presenting an argument
- ✦ using examples of the text to justify an argument
- ✦ use of reference anthologies
- ✦ use inference and deduction
- ✦ comparing with other poems
- ✦ recognising author style
- ✦ write in similar style
- ✦ write a parody

UNDERSTANDING

Poetry:
- ✦ encompasses a wide range of types
- ✦ does not have to rhyme
- ✦ can have a structured or free form
- ✦ followed strict rules in the past
- ✦ sometimes follow rules today
- ✦ is a powerful force in the media
- ✦ can be narrative
- ✦ can be purely descriptive
- ✦ is a traditional form in many cultures
- ✦ can provide primary historical evidence
- ✦ is for everyone
- ✦ can demonstrate the power of language
- ✦ can be a very flexible play material
- ✦ can be written in dialects
- ✦ can use standard forms of language
- ✦ language is constantly changing.

CONTROL AND POWER OF LANGUAGE

Feeling comfortable and confident about poetry can be an empowering experience for children. Knowing that they have the ability to read, understand and express their personal views about poems can bring competency to their own use of language, not only in their writing of poetry but also in other areas of their language work.

INTEREST IN AND ENJOYMENT OF LANGUAGE WORK

Research shows that high performance is directly linked to high motivation. Enjoyment and interest are prime motivating factors in Junior classrooms, and there is much to be enjoyed and explored in working with poetry. We cannot afford to assume, however, that all the children in our class do enjoy poetry. What we can do is ensure that the poetry work in our classrooms is carefully planned with enjoyment and interest in mind. In this way, our children can experience the pleasure and stimulation that is undoubtedly possible with poetry work.

WHICH POETRY?

A varied yet balanced diet of poetry in the Junior classroom is important. Some suggestions are made here about how teachers can begin to equip themselves with the best tools for the job of teaching poetry in their classrooms.

CHECK THE STOCK IN YOUR READING CORNER

Children will not read poetry independently and collaboratively if there is no poetry for them to read. The quality of the books available to children will directly affect their attitudes to reading as well as their reading development, so classroom and school library stock needs to be monitored and evaluated regularly. There is no escape from the fact that budgets in schools are tight. All the more reason why the selection and purchase of books in schools must be carefully planned and prioritised. At least 10 per cent of books in a classroom reading corner should be poetry books.

START TO BUILD YOUR OWN COLLECTION OF POETRY FOR READING TO THE CLASS

Children's beliefs and feelings about poetry are likely to be a direct reflection of the poetry on their teacher's bookshelf. If they only ever hear extracts from one, inappropriate anthology they will react accordingly. Books such as *Poetry 0–16* (Styles and Triggs, 1988) which list and describe anthologies and collections, and *The New Where's That Poem?* (Morris, 1992) which is a reference guide to poems listed thematically are real treasures in assisting you to find what you need. It is also a good idea to treat yourself to a browse in a good bookshop or public library in order to extend your personal knowledge of what is available. (See the list of titles opposite.)

CHOOSE A WIDE RANGE OF POETRY

Whether choosing books to read to the children or for the reading corner, it is important to ensure that there is a wide selection. If we are to open up children's views about poetry and celebrate the diversity of poetic language, we will need to expose them to that diversity. The check-list opposite is by no means definitivee, but is intended as a 'starter pack' of poetry book suggestions, one from each of thirteen categories.

HOW CAN POETRY BE TAUGHT?

Careful planning is needed in order to give children their true entitlement to an enriching poetry curriculum. This needs to include a long-term overview as well as the short-term action plans. A sudden half-term stint of poetry in isolation is of limited value if the children are unused to working within a poetic framework. In the same way, the sudden introduction of a single session poetry writing activity perhaps because it represents one in a list of writing genres for the term, is going to reap fewer rewards than a two-week poetry writing focus which builds on previous preparation and experience. If the discrete poetry plans are to work well, they need to take place

Category	Title	Year	Author	Publisher
City poems	Our Lives	1988	Strathclyde Young People	Third Eye Centre, Glasgow
Classic poems	The Books of a Thousand Poems	1990	Anthology	Unwin Hyman
Festival poems	Let's Celebrate	1989	John Foster	Oxford University Press
Funny poems	The Kingfisher Book of Comic Verse	1986	Roger McGough (Ed.)	Faber and Faber
Games and chants	Twiddling Your Thumbs	1988	Wendy Cope	Kingfisher
General anthologies	Poetry	1992	Wes McGee	Scholastic Ltd
Modern poets	Two's Company	1992	Jackie Kay	Penguin
Multi-cultural poems	A Caribbean Dozen	1994	Agard and Nichols (Eds)	Walker Books
Regional poetry	Poems in the Lancashire Dialect	1974	Louisa Bearman	Dalesman Books
School poems	Please Mrs Butler	1983	Allan Ahlberg	Penguin
Songs	Apusskidu	1975	Beatrice Harrop	A & C Black Ltd
Shakespeare	A Midsummer Night's Dream	1992	Leon Garfield	Heinemann
War poetry	In Time of War	1987	Anne Harvey (Ed.)	Blackie

against a backdrop of familiarity and confidence acquired through ongoing and regular contributions. These might include cross-curricular approaches to poetry in addition to systematic discrete exposure.

It is also extremely important that primary teachers do not fall into the trap of providing arduous lessons involving complex analyses which are going to kill the children's enthusiasm and interest. Rather, they need to plan activities which are going to draw the children into the poem through active involvement and exploration. The plans for poetry need to take account of where the children are at in terms of their understanding of poetry as well as opportunities for thematic approaches relating to other work in the classroom. It is not merely the activities themselves which contribute towards children's poetic awareness, the classroom environment also makes a contribution. This includes the resources, the rules of access to those resources and the attitude of the teacher. Children are, for example, unlikely to choose to read poetry alone during a period of silent reading unless:

✦ there are poetry books to choose from;

✦ they are actively encouraged to choose them;

✦ their motivation has been inspired by an enthusiastic teacher (or parent), who regularly reads poetry aloud.

The following list of questions is offered to assist and support teachers in their planning and preparation of poetry.

✦ Do I read poetry aloud to the class regularly?

✦ Have I introduced new material regularly as well as old favourites?

✦ Is there a sufficiently wide range of poetry books in the reading corner?

✦ Does this represent the range of reading abilities in my class?

✦ Have I included poems on any of the classroom displays?

✦ Have we made a display of poetry books and poets in the reading corner recently?

✦ Is it possible to invite a poet to visit our classroom?

✦ Can I show the children any video material of poets at work?
✦ Have I provided opportunities:
  ✦ to read independently?
  ✦ to read in pairs and groups?
  ✦ to perform poetry?
✦ How can I link reading with writing activities?

The following list of activities provides a range of starting points which concentrate particularly on the reading rather than the writing of poetry. (Writing is included on the list as it is obviously one of the ways in which children are going to develop their understanding.) It is hoped that these starting points will provide an initial stimulus framework for planning.

TYPES OF ACTIVITIES

Discussion as a whole class
Discussion in groups or pairs using prompt cards
Reading aloud with gaps for others to guess
Exploration through drama
Favourite poem spot – child reads to class instead of teacher
Poetry workshop with guest poet
Poetry week (like a Bookweek).
Small group activities
Discussion in small groups with and without the teacher
Performing a poem by exploring the sound (volume, pitch, rhythm, speed, etc.)
Presenting information charts
Poetry research (for example finding a relevant poem to include in topic work)
Pair work
Creating a word collage from favourite words in a poem
Thesaurus games (for example using thesaurus to substitute words then spot the difference)
Writing in the style of a poem
Writing on the same theme as a selection of poems
Presenting storyboards
Individual work

Cloze procedure (teacher designed and pupil designed)
Plotting rhyme-schemes and then using these for own writing
Highlighting vocabulary on photocopies (for example the rhyming words, or adjectives)
Cutting up the text and inserting new ideas
Changing some of the words
Changing the ending or the beginning
Changing the tense
Presenting the poem in pictorial form
Painting an abstract response
Drawing a picture of the poem then inserting chosen vocabulary from the poem
Illustrating certain lines or sections
Poetry reviews

DEVELOPING A WHOLE SCHOOL POLICY

Policies need to be useful to teachers by informing, supporting and guiding their work in a way which is in tune with the other teachers in the school. Children benefit through a well-balanced and developmental approach to their learning. The inclusion of poetry guidelines in a language policy can prove an invaluable support to teachers.

The poetry section of a language policy would normally include an agreed belief system about the value of poetry in school. This would be followed by a description of agreed teaching approaches and a rationale for those approaches. Specific guidelines might then be produced for each year band. The Poetry Policy Triangle below offers some areas for which group descriptions could be produced.

key skills
key concepts
key understanding
poetry forms for writing
aspects of teaching reading
resourcing in the book corner
suggested anthologies for teachers to read aloud
contexts for poetry, including discrete and cross-curricular approaches

So, for example, a column about figurative language (understanding) might look like this:

Year 1   use single descriptive words on collage and pictures

Year 2   explore and use descriptive words in their own poems

Year 3   explore and use alliteration and onomatopoeia

Year 4   understand the meaning of *adjective* and *adverb*; use and identify these

Year 5   explore and use *simile*

Year 6   explore and use *metaphor*, consolidation and further exploration of *imagery*

NB Children should learn the terminology in italics in addition to exploring the meaning.

DIFFERENTIATION AND PROGRESSION

When planning an overall programme of poetry for a class of children, teachers have to take into consideration the range of challenges needed by those children. Even an all Year 6 class can quite feasibly cover four or even five different ability levels for reading. If children are to feel confident in their learning and are to develop through a clear succession of progressive stages they must be allowed to work at the right level. Equally important is the fact that this level must be one in a whole series of levels which gradually build upon each other in an appropriate and meaningful way. This can seem like quite a daunting task, particularly in an area like poetry where there are virtually no progressive schemes published (as there are in maths for instance) to guide teachers through a relevant pathway in their planning. If children are faced with unsuitable activities and inappropriate material, they are likely to be put off poetry and may even start to believe some of the myths listed earlier.

DIFFERENTIATING ACTIVITIES IN THE CLASSROOM

Clearly, the framework outlined above cannot be presented as a whole class level in practice because there will be children in every class who will be behind or ahead of such plans. The guidelines therefore represent a basic core for each year group, but can also be used as a model for differentiation. For example, a group of less able pupils in Year 6 would benefit from consolidating earlier work on adjectives and adverbs than from moving on to sophisticated exploration of metaphor. Once there is a clear framework for progression in place it makes it much easier to differentiate classroom activities. The two go hand in hand!

Five Haiku

Tantrums of flame gush
from throats of gunpowder tubes.
Take notice of me!

Bones of bonfire shift.
Startled sparks light up skull-eyed
faces in bushes.

Wisp of grey veil floats,
like some weary Guy Fawkes' ghost,
out through night's black walls.
Spent sparklers spear out
in webs of wire weaponry
at anxious ankles.

High over midnight
an insistent arc of stars,
still stage-struck, signs off.
Gina Douthwaite
(from Let's Celebrate—Festival Poems)

Having read the poem two or three times, made a response and discussed it with the whole class, this poem could be explored on several levels by different groups. These might include:

✦ illustrating verse two, then adding further adjectives and similes;

✦ highlighting (with felt tips) the adjectives throughout the poem – changing them for new ones;

✦ highlighting (with felt tips) the examples of alliteration – writing an additional haiku with particular emphasis on alliteration;

✦ comparison of simile and metaphor – writing an additional haiku with particular emphasis on metaphor.

This model has a common starting point, but there are many models of differentiation, and sometimes different groups might be given different poems for different purposes.

SUMMARY

Poetry has an important part to play in Junior classrooms, and yet there are many pitfalls. An awareness of negative attitudes to poetry can assist with promoting enthusiasm and motivation. This has to be done through careful planning, good quality resources and a varied range of interesting and purposeful activities. These activities should meet the needs of all ability levels and should follow a progressive pathway. These elements operate at their very best when teachers demonstrate their own enthusiasm and pleasure. Confidence to do this will grow through a well-informed, professional knowledge of poetry and poets, and a clear school policy which offers systematic guidance. The result will be children who are competently developing skills, knowledge and understanding to a diversity of language, and who can enjoy the vast rewards which poetry has to offer.

REFERENCES

Agard, J. and Nichols, G. (Eds) (1994) *A Caribbean Dozen*, Walker Books.

Foster, J. (1989) *Let's Celebrate – Festival Poems*, OUP.

Harvey, A. (1987) *In Time of War*, Puffin

Lancashire Life (Eds) (1975) *Just Sithabod*, Whitehorn Press.

Morris, H. (1992) *The New Where's That Poem?* Simon & Schuster.

Styles, M and Triggs, P. (1988) *Poetry 0–16*, Books for Keeps.

Scholastic Poetry boxes (1990) *The Book of a Thousand Poems*, Unwin Hyman.

VIDEO

(1994) *Count to Five and Stay Alive – The Poetry*, Team Video Productions.

(1994) *Count to Five and Stay Alive – The Workshop*, Team Video Productions.

These are available from: Team Video Productions, Canalot 222, Kensal Rd., London, W10 5BN.

FURTHER READING

Brown, B. and Glass, M. (1991) *Important Words*, Heinemann.

Corbett, B. and Moses, B. (1986) *Caterpaults and Kingfishers – Teaching Poetry in Primary Schools*, OUP.

Corbett, P. and Moses, B. (1989) *Poetry for Projects*, Scholastic Ltd.

Orme, D. (1992) *The Essential Guide to Poetry*, Folens.

Rosen, M. (1994) *Count to Five and Say I'm Alive – The Words*, Team Video Productions

Yates, I. (1991) *Let's Investigate Writing Poetry*, Scholastic Ltd.

CHAPTER 4

TEACHING READING THROUGH DRAMA

If children are to become active and responsive readers, they will need a sound understanding and knowledge of how they can relate to texts when reading independently. Therefore, if we expect our pupils to develop and use such skills when they read alone, it is only fair that we teach them how to do this. Drama is an ideal medium to achieve this aim. The rich range of texts demanded by the National Curriculum offer myriad ways of working, beyond the mere dramatisation of stories. These can be used with children before, during and after drama activities and examples of these are discussed.

Good organisation, clear aims and an active style of teaching are crucial to the quality and success of good drama activities. These issues are discussed with practical examples of ideas which might be tried.

WHY USE DRAMA TO DEVELOP READING SKILLS?

The National Curriculum reading requirements for Key Stage 2 encompass a broad range of interactive processes which reflect the complex nature of reading. It is clear that, as children are developing as readers, they are also developing as thinkers, moving towards more abstract, critical and interpretative modes of thought. Similarly, children's feelings and responses are developing and changing, and opportunities should be provided for them to explore and express these in a safe and productive environment. It is unrealistic to suggest that children should do this by sitting silently with their reading books.

If children are to develop sophisticated and creative responses to texts they need opportunities to explore these processes through practical, interactive activities. Drama can allow this to happen. Listed below are some examples of interactive processes (related to reading) which can be explored through drama:

- empathising
- judging
- recalling
- retelling
- re-enacting
- criticising
- justifying
- explaining
- predicting
- experiencing
- imagining
- comparing
- discussing
- pretending
- interpreting
- analysing
- describing
- questioning
- answering
- exploring
- evaluating
- finding out

THE VALUE OF DRAMA AS A LEARNING METHOD

During the 1960s and 1970s, educational drama enjoyed respected acknowledgement of its value in schools. Theories of child-centred education and the significance of experiential learning were at their zenith, providing a relevant contextual backdrop to the active growth of drama as an effective and worthwhile activity. The work of proponents such as Peter Slade, Gavin Bolton and Dorothy Heathcote provided well-documented evidence of drama as a valuable tool for teaching and learning. The inclusion of drama in teacher training courses and the more frequent appearance of drama in primary school curricula confirmed the importance of the medium, both as a subject in its own right and as a pedagogical approach.

The end of the 1980s marked a sea-change in the arts, as a more content-based curriculum was introduced into schools, accompanied by a trend towards more formal styles of teaching. The pressures of an overloaded curriculum with externally imposed requirements for schools meant that drama became increasingly marginalised as a subject, and the pedagogical rationale for using this style of teaching seemed also to disappear.

In 1990, HMI reported that:

> Only a minority of primary schools have a well-developed policy and guide-lines for their work in drama. Consequently drama rarely receives consistent attention either as a means of enriching work in other subjects or as an activity in its own right.

The report was based on inspections of 285 primary schools in England between 1982 and 1986. It identified 30 schools which exemplified good practice in drama in order to cite useful illustrations of sound educational practice. One important summary point was that, where it was done well, drama had

> a strong influence upon the development of language and literacy.

The role of drama in oracy is self-evident, but its potential to develop children as readers and writers has been less exploited in the past. The Final Orders for the Teaching of English in the National Curriculum (1995) state that:

> opportunities for reading should include both independent and shared reading of play scripts and other texts, by group and the whole class.

Reflecting this need for an interactive approach to language learning it is therefore appropriate that teachers are encouraged to include drama techniques in their schemes of work across the curricula. Close scrutiny of science, history and geography documents provides hope of a new wave for drama as a suggested method of teaching. Teachers should recognise drama as an invaluable method in their teaching repertoire rather than regarding it as yet another bolt-on addition to a crammed schedule.

In education, drama is distinct from theatre, although the two can sometimes meet at various points along a continuum. Educational drama and theatre represent the two extremes of such a continuum. Educational drama is an active learning experience which is for the benefit of the pupil. Theatre is performance-driven and is for the benefit of an audience. However, in school there are times when performance and sharing of work are an important part of the drama, although this is not always appropriate.(See diagram below)

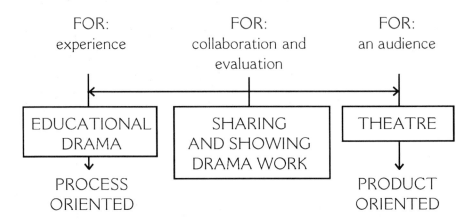

Drama is an experiential process which is not necessarily intended to be performed for an audience and is, therefore, not subject to time-consuming repetition and practice. It encompasses a wide variety of ways of working in which children are actively engaged. Drama can deliver content from many subject areas which may be explored and experienced actively rather than received passively. Examples of the range of activities and the cross-curricular contexts are explored in detail later in this Chapter.

A MODEL OF INTERACTION BETWEEN DRAMA AND READING

The National Curriculum requirements for reading are of an active rather than a passive nature. Children are required to respond and relate to a wide variety of texts. They need to read for a range of purposes, and employ different reading skills at different times. They are required to develop a knowledge of literature along with the confidence to express their own views. They need to be efficient and selective in the retrieval of information from different sources. Such requirements demand interactive modes of learning, and drama is the ideal medium for many activities which will extend and develop pupils as readers.

The model presented here demonstrates a theory of the relationship between drama and reading which is designed to promote what has been called 'The Evolution of the Reader'.

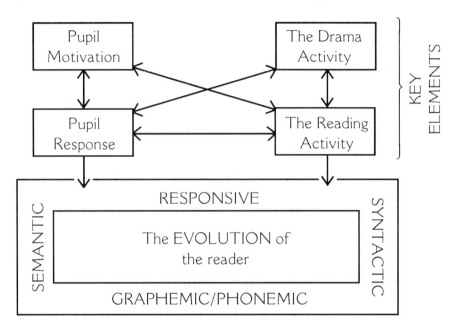

The 'Evolution of the Reader' represents an organic and wholesome growth of the developmental processes of four main operations of reading – graphemic/phonemic, syntactic, semantic and responsive. These four operations of reading develop simultaneously, although not necessarily at the same rates. At Key Stage 2, graphemic/phonemic awareness and syntactic competence are, for the majority of pupils well established, whilst semantic operations cannot always be assumed. The responsive capabilities of older readers will have been developed to a range of levels, but will now be ripe for a more rapid rate of growth. The evolutionary process is the unfolding of the reader into an increasingly complex creature and takes place from babyhood to adulthood.

The model illustrates how drama can be a significant contributing factor to the evolutionary process for Junior readers. It illustrates four inter-related elements which are significant to the process and have been named the 'Key Elements'. These are:

• the reading activity i.e. the pupil, text and purpose, for example scanning for information;

• pupil response i.e. consequence of reading, for example following an instruction, empathising;

• pupil motivation i.e. the pupil's level of willingness or enthusiasm;

• the drama activity i.e. the context and vehicle for the reading.

THE READING ACTIVITY

It is clear to all that children will not evolve as readers unless they read! As illustrated by the model, experience of reading is contributing directly to the evolutionary process. This experience will provide opportunities to learn and practise the different operations listed earlier (included in the 'Evolution' box of the model). However, at Junior level, there is a considerable shift towards independent reading and this can sometimes mean that the reader is left to cope alone without the necessary skills to get the best out of the activity. The reading might take place without the level of sophistication increasing. In many cases, the reading does not take place because the child has lost interest or simply can't be bothered.

THE PUPIL RESPONSE

The response operation has been separated out for the purposes of the model because it is considered to be the most appropriate aspect of reading to be developed through drama. Pupil response is considered to be the least likely operation to evolve directly from independent reading activities. Drama addresses the socially interactive nature of response, facilitating discussion, exploration and debate. This discrete inclusion of reader response in the model highlights the fact that this is a major area for development, although as texts are read, other skills are sometimes addressed.

PUPIL MOTIVATION

Lack of motivation to read is regularly identified by teachers as a significant problem with older primary school children. This sometimes manifests itself in the form of poor knowledge of authors, reluctance to try something new, or professed boredom with books. If teachers are to continue assisting the evolutionary process, they need to ensure that their children are motivated to read.

THE DRAMA ACTIVITY

In sharp contrast, drama is usually extremely popular with most children – lessons are characterised by enthusiasm, energy and commitment. Such a positive approach to this type of learning can be harnessed to deliver an exciting and productive approach to reading development.

AT WHAT POINT DO READING AND DRAMA MEET?

The two most traditional ways of relating drama and reading have been the reading and enactment of play scripts, and the narration and enactment of stories. These should not be dismissed, as there are obvious values particularly in relation to the semantics of reading. It is important to consider other points at which the relationship between texts and drama activities can meet.

These can be divided into three categories:

PRE-DRAMA READING

In this relationship, the text provides the starting point for the drama, and the drama provides the vehicle for in-depth exploration of the text. Examples of this might include:
• developing alternative endings;
• developing imagined scenes based on inference;

- character motivation (for example thought bubbles);
- court scene;
- debate;
- action from another's perspective;
- defence of a character's actions;
- interview with a character;
- challenging subject matter to be explored.

READING DURING THE DRAMA

This way of working uses texts as an integral part of the drama activity. This is a particularly appropriate use for texts which are new to the children so that they have to 'interrogate the text' actively in order to understand and participate in the activity. Examples of this might include:

- following instructions;
- presenting the news;
- documentary evidence;
- two sides to the story;
- sound effects;
- use of vocabulary;
- tableaux of scenes;
- narration and mime;
- movement sequence of feelings;
- using information books to create a simulation;
- responses to letter or report;
- changing story structures;
- exploration of dialects.

READING AS EXTENSION OR DEVELOPMENT AFTER THE DRAMA

In this context, texts can be introduced after the drama activity in order to build on what has happened beforehand. This could happen back in the classroom as a follow-up activity or as an extension of the actual drama project. Examples of this might include:

- using the drama to prepare for a new text;

- using the drama to simulate a descriptive passage or poem which is introduced to the children afterwards;
- using the drama to introduce the children to an experience which is, developed afterwards through reading;
- subsequent research on a theme or subject;
- comparative reading;
- anthology research on the same theme;
- reading each other's responses to the drama;
- reading and responding to each other's scripts;
- writing and reading alternatives;
- further information on challenging issues.

By considering these different places in which texts can be integrated, teachers have the facility to introduce a whole range of reading challenges to their children within an exciting and motivating context.

TYPES OF TEXTS AND RELATED ACTIVITIES

The National Curriculum makes it quite clear that children at Key Stage 2 should have the opportunity to encounter a wide range of texts. When planning schemes of work, it is important to identify where the provision of such a range might take place without introducing de-contextualised and inappropriate activities. Drama presents teachers with the potential to provide relevant and engaging contexts in which children can engage with a rich variety of reading materials.

In addition to children's books, there are many texts which are not designed specifically for children – texts which are used in our daily lives such as leaflets, brochures, catalogues and instruction booklets. Indeed, it can help children to develop a real sense of purpose and high self-esteem as readers if they are given such texts to use in the classroom.

FICTION

Fiction can be explored and understood on many levels. Not only can children be helped to understand the construction, style and presentation of texts, but they should also be encouraged to consider ideas, issues and themes. They need to develop the confidence to discuss and justify their own opinions so that they may evaluate what they read. Sometimes this will be through relating what they read to their own experiences, and sometimes through making comparisons with other texts.

Drama provides children with the opportunity to empathise with fictional characters and explore and experience stories. It provides a vehicle for construction and reconstruction, statement and imagination, reading the lines and reading between the lines.

ACTIVITY 1: HUGHES, T. (1993) THE IRON WOMAN, FABER & FABER.

Debate the issues of chemical waste disposal.
Mime 'the scream' using descriptive vocabulary from the text.
Interview those who work at the chemical factory.

ACTIVITY 2: FINE, A. (1989) GOGGLE EYES, PENGUIN.

Use the flashback technique.
Improvise arguments with parents.
Improvise a group of parents discussing their children.

ACTIVITY 3: BURNINGHAM, J. (1988) GRANPA, PUFFIN.

Examine the structure of the text.
Look at the significance of inference and prediction.
Create a new story in tableau form.

POETRY

Not only can poetry be rich in figurative language, it can also present ideas which challenge opinions and emotions. Exploration of poetry through drama can produce rich results in terms of analysis and interpretation. Classic poetry can provide interesting models of language and powerful stories. Historical analysis and comparisons can also be usefully drawn from the classics.

ACTIVITY 1: KAY, J. (1994) 'DUNCAN GETS EXPELLED FROM SCHOOL' FROM TWO'S COMPANY, PENGUIN.

There are three big boys from primary seven
who wait at the main school gate with stones
in their teeth and names in their pockets.
Every day the three big boys are waiting.
'There she is. Into her boys. Hey Sambo.'

I dread the bell ringing, and the walk home.
My best friend is scared of them and runs off.
Some days they shove a mud pie into my mouth.
'That's what you should eat,' and make me eat it.
Then they all look in my mouth, prodding a stick.

I'm always hoping we get detention.
I'd love to write 'I will be better' 400 times.
The things I do? I pull Agnes MacNamara's hair.
Or put a ruler under Rhona's bum and ping it back
till she screams; or I make myself sick in the toilet.

Until the day the headmaster pulls me out,
asking all about the three big boys.
I'm scared to open my mouth.
Be he says, 'you can tell me, is it true?'
So out it comes, making me eat the mud pies.

Two of them got lines for the whole of May.
But he got expelled that Duncan MacKay.

Groups of six might work on three tableaux depicting a story about bullying or racism with connecting spoken narrative. The discussion and planning which would need to take place would provide a valuable learning process in itself, and the tableaux produced create powerful images of the theme. Role play activities in which the experiences of a victim are explored can produce powerful identification, empathy and discussion. This type of drama needs to be planned by teachers who are confident with this way of working with children who are familiar and comfortable with the drama mode.

PLAYS

There are many play scripts written for classrooms, as the genre becomes ever more popular with children. Scripted plays can be used in various ways. The worst scenario is the repeated practice and rehearsal of lines aloud and the best allows active exploration of character motivation and action to take place. Similarly, children can benefit enormously from having the opportunity to intervene in texts by adding lines of their own, planning extra scenes, introducing additional characters, creating alternative endings. All of these activities have the potential to probe the realms of inference and imagination.

Classic plays can also provide rich sources of material, particularly for the more able readers. George Bernard Shaw's *Pygmalion* (Penguin) is a good choice for the examination of dialects and social issues. Remember that extracts are sometimes sufficient to produce a worthwhile activity. These may whet the appetite of more voracious readers, whilst providing a self-contained resource for the activity itself.

The enjoyment of Shakespeare in the Junior years can pay dividends later in terms of children's confidence as well as their knowledge and understanding. All too often, secondary pupils are faced with works of Shakespeare for the first time and are daunted by the recognised greatness, and fears about the academic elitism of these works which seem to permeate large sections of our society. There is no doubt that reading the plays in their complete form at an early age would almost certainly guarantee a total rejection or resistance. Listening to the stories, however, (there are many versions: Miles, B. (1986) *Favourite Tales from Shakespeare*, Hamlyn; Garfield, L. (1985) *Shakespeare Stories*, Gollancz; Garfield, L. (1992) *Shakespeare The Animated Tales*, Heinemann) and playing with parts of these can build firm foundations for later learning.

TEACHING READING THROUGH DRAMA

ACTIVITY 1: LAMB, C. AND M. (1987) 'A MIDSUMMER NIGHT'S DREAM' FROM TALES FROM SHAKESPEARE, PUFFIN.

Tell the Lamb's Tales version of the Pyramus and Thisbe section of A Midsummer Night's Dream. Ask the children to recreate the story in their own words. Examine the original text. Ask them to see if they can include a minimum of three original lines into their own version.

NON-FICTION

Non-fiction texts are widely used in classrooms, particularly for topic work. At its best, reading non-fiction involves a range of skills (see Chapter 2) and results in clear understanding. Evaluation and comparisons of books on the same subject are also an important aspect of this type of reading. Use of non-fiction works well where children are required to interpret information and refer. to it in a different format. In this way they are absorbing, manipulating and applying the information acquired. This process ensures a much deeper level of understanding, not only of the content, but also of the form and organisation of non-fiction texts. Drama offers various ways to extract and apply information from non-fiction texts.

ACTIVITY 1: VIKING TABLEAUX

Create three tableau scenes to represent a Viking longship, a Viking banquet and a Viking burial. Make the non-fiction books available for reference so that the children can seek actual information to include in the scenes. The scenes must be based on evidence from the books, rather than impressionistic fantasy. After showing the tableaux to the rest of the class, encourage the children to talk about how they used the books, how they found the relevant information and which books were most useful and why.

ACTIVITY 2: A DOCUMENTARY OR INTERVIEW

Researching a significant scientist (for example Marie Curie) in order to present a documentary or an interview. Drama, in this instance, does not require a large space; three children could work on this project in the classroom, perhaps as part of an

PRIMARY
PROFESSIONAL BOOKSHELF
97

integrated session whilst other activities are taking place. This would also solve the problem of not having enough books for the whole class.

REFERENCE

This is a separate category because it encompasses a range of texts beyond non-fiction including:

- telephone directories;
- Yellow Pages;
- encyclopaedias;
- dictionaries;
- thesauruses;
- CD-Roms;
- Guinness Book of Records;
- timetables;
- travel brochures.

Using these kinds of texts develops children's retrieval skills by: alphabetical process, posing a retrieval strategy, reading for meaning and using the information. Drama can create enjoyable contexts for children to practise using such skills. It is perfectly valid to have a role-play corner in a Junior classroom, and yet they are rarely seen. Dressing up clothes, artefacts and a novelty environment can be very exciting for today's children, who play less and less as TV and computers dominate their lives. Such a corner can be used effectively as part of normal classroom activities providing that the children are given guidance.

ACTIVITY 1: SET UP A TRAVEL AGENT'S SHOP

Involve the children in the design of a travel agent's shop and provide a vast quantity of brochures, papers, writing materials, cheque books, toy money, office equipment, and (if at all possible) import your classroom computer to set up a database. Allow the children to role-play in pairs, providing them with the facilities to look for and book a holiday. Travel brochures are incredibly complex, with cross referencing being a major feature; flight times, for example, are usually at the back of the brochure. Evidence of this activity could be a completed holiday application form and personalised airline tickets, requiring the children to discover and collate a complex range of data.

This information could be included in the children's topic books. The activity could, justifiably, contribute to geography work or even a topic on environments. The content would be relevant to the topic, and the reading skills would be a valuable part of the children's developing work in language.

ACTIVITY 2: WORD GAMES

The children work in groups of four. The teacher gives them a word on a card. They use a thesaurus to find a suitable alternative, then make up a one-minute scene in which the alternative word is spoken. When the scenes are planned, they perform them to the rest of the class, having first shown the card with the original word. The rest of the class have to guess the replacement word.

LEISURE TEXTS

Everyday life in our society brings us face to face with an ever increasing variety of leisure texts. There are a multiplicity of newspapers and magazines.

Comics are a good starting-point for development activities, and this genre should not be dismissed simply because it is a child-centred literacy. The construction and content of comics can raise many issues which provide a rich source for discussion and evaluation.

When teachers use leisure texts they acknowledge the wider world of literacy beyond the classroom. This is a literacy which is quite often a feature of the children's home lives and therefore a good foundation on which to build further reading skills.

ACTIVITY 1: NEWSPAPER REPORT

Working in groups of four, the children are given a page of a local newspaper from which they should choose an article which interests them. They then prepare to report on this from the viewpoints of four different people. For example, a car accident from the point of view of the driver, the police, a witness, and the injured party.

ACTIVITY 2: TV GUIDE

Working in groups of four give each group a copy of a TV guide. Ask them to choose one particular time and day of the week. Each child represents a programme from a different channel and has to justify why the rest of the class should watch their programme rather than the other three.

COMMERCIAL TEXTS

We live in a print-laden society in which it is impossible not to be faced with texts of one kind or another. Many are available at no cost whatsoever, and it is well worth scouring shops and other public locations for free texts which can be used for interesting and useful activities in school. Look for:

* circulars;
* advertising;
* leaflets;
* junk mail;
* packaging;
* tourist information;
* supermarket fliers;
* catalogues.

ACTIVITY 1: ROLE PLAY CORNER – TOURIST INFORMATION OFFICE

This activity can be resourced with the free material which is readily available from local advisory centres. In groups of three or four, the children hold a planning meeting at the 'office' during which they have to plan and cost an itinerary for a one-day coach tour for senior citizens. They must plan routes, visits and costings, and the evidence of their work will be produced on relevant forms, cross-referenced to pages in brochures, leaflets and transport guides.

ACTIVITY 2: JUNK MAIL DRAMA

Make a collection (with the permission of parents) of all the 'junk mail' which comes through the children's letterboxes during a two-week period. Then, working in groups of four, children select a letter from the pile of junk mail and construct a story about how it changed one family's lives. Much of the valuable reading which takes place will be during the collection of the mail, and in the decision-making process when they choose the letter for the story. The teacher should facilitate discussion about the rights and wrongs of junk-mail, the issues involved, and the various formats used by companies.

DOCUMENTS

Documents can include:
- archive material;
- planning applications;
- old letters;
- school reports;
- historical documents;
- minutes of meetings;
- government reports;
- legal documents;
- local council documents.

These texts are particularly useful for encouraging children to read for meaning and to draw out information for a specific purpose. Drama can assist this process by relating the texts to the real situations from which they have arisen.

ACTIVITY 1: COUNCIL MEETING

Try to obtain documents from your local council relating to planning permission so that the children can experience this type of text. Create a hypothetical application of your own to distribute to the children. This should be of a controversial nature, for example, the building of a new road across allotments. The children should be organised so that they represent different groups from the town. They will need to prepare their arguments. Other texts might be used at this stage for reference and information. A 'meeting' can then be held at which views are debated. The teacher would be in role as the chair of the meeting.

ACTIVITY 2: LIFE AS AN EVACUEE

It is possible to trace letters from evacuees either in museums (the Imperial War Museum is a useful source), or from older relatives or members of the community. Local newspapers may help to procure such materials. Having given the children copies of the documents ask them to reconstruct some of the scenes described. Inferential comprehension can also be practised to develop the fact into fiction.

MANAGEMENT OF DRAMA ACTIVITIES

If teachers are to feel confident working with drama activities, they need to have clear aims and plans for their lessons. Although drama sessions are often noisy and busy, they need to be well structured and carefully prepared. There are some pointers to guide teachers on their way.

THERE IS NO ONE METHOD OF TEACHING DRAMA

There are many experiences which teachers can provide for their children within a drama session. Different modes and group sizes can be employed according to the nature of the work involved. Some examples are:

- Pair-work (for example interviews);
- Spontaneous improvisation;
- Planned improvisation;
- Mime;
- Movement sequences;
- Tableaux;
- Whole class role-play (teacher in role);
- Whole class simulation (teacher in role);
- Class interrogating a 'visitor' (child or teacher in role);
- Story scenes;
- Play in role-play corner.

A LARGE SPACE IS NOT ALWAYS REQUIRED

In schools where hall space is at a premium, it is well worth taking five minutes to clear tables and chairs away so that you can use your own classroom space. Some modes of drama, however, can take place in the normal classroom set-up. Pair work and interviewing can happen with the whole class simultaneously. In a classroom where the management model is one of simultaneous activities, a group can easily be working on a drama project in one corner of the room. The role-play corner works well in this scenario.

TIMING

As with all classroom activities, it is important to consider the timing of activities carefully. Prolonged work can lead to off-task distractions. Set goals clearly so that the children understand exactly what is expected of them within the stated time scales.

PERFORMANCE

The theatrical approach of repeated rehearsal is inappropriate in an educational setting where time is in short supply. The processes of the drama are usually more valuable in terms of learning than the end-product. That end-product is, however, often evidence of the process and is usually extremely important to the children. It is sometimes appropriate for groups to show their work to just one other group, or for pairs to tell their story to another pair, rather than have each group performing to the whole class. In this way, time is saved, but the children feel fulfilled in the sharing of their work.

TEACHER EVALUATION AND ASSESSMENT

Drama time is often a wonderful opportunity for teachers to observe their children at work. A well planned drama lesson will mean that children are absorbed and totally involved in their activity – they often forget that the teacher is even there! Circulating and observing during group work time can enable teachers to make notes and assessments. As with all types of assessment teachers should be clear what learning outcomes they are looking for, for example, understanding that the main character's perspective is not necessarily the same as other characters involved in the action. Observations during drama can also provide teachers with an invaluable source of information of the unexpected kind — how children work together, and their perceptions of what is read.

SUMMARY

Drama enables children to explore a wide range of texts within many contexts, encompassing English and other areas of the curriculum. The value and power of this has been illustrated by a model in which reading activities, drama activities, pupil response and pupil motivation are apparently inter-connected. It has been argued that the dynamics between these four can make a major contribution to how pupils 'evolve' as readers.

The examples and issues discussed in this chapter are in no way intended to provide a definitive guide to the use of drama in schools. Rather they are intended to extend an awareness of how useful the method can be as a tool for learning, and specifically how this can relate to the development of reading with Junior pupils. There are many ways in which drama can be taught and further reading will be needed by those who feel motivated to introduce drama into their teaching repertoire. Nevertheless, it is hoped that the concept of translating reader response into action learning in order to develop and expand the understanding of reading skills is one which will appeal to teachers enough for them to give it a try. The results can be rewarding and satisfy pupils and teachers alike.

REFERENCES

Bolton, G. (1984) *Drama as Education: an argument for placing drama at the centre of the curriculum*, Longman.
Davis, D. and Lawrence, C. (eds) (1986) *Gavin Bolton: Selected Writing*, Longman.
DFE (1995) *English in the National Curriculum*, HMSO.
HMI (1990) *The Teaching and Learning of Drama*, HMSO.
Johnson, L. and O'Neill, C. (eds) (1984) *Dorothy Heathcote:*

Collected writings on education and drama, Hutchinson.

Kay, J. (1992) *Two's Company,* Puffin Books.

Slade, P. (1970) *An Introduction to Child Drama,* University of London Press.

FURTHER READING

Crinson, J. and Leak, L. (eds) (1993) *Move Back the Desks,* NATE.

O'Neill, C. and Lambert, A. (1990) *Drama Structures,* Heinemann.

Readman, G. and Lamont, G. (1994) *Drama. A Handbook for Primary Teachers,* BBC.

Somers, J. (1994) *Drama in the Curriculum,* Cassell.

Woolland, B. (1993) *The Teaching of Drama in the Primary School,* Longman.

CHAPTER 5

A MULTI-MEDIA APPROACH TO TEACHING READING

Media variety - magazines, TV, radio, computers - is very much a part of most children's lives these days. The twentieth century has witnessed a most dramatic technological growth in communication. That growth has extended from telegraphs to fax machines, from gramophones to CDs, from computers to Multi-media packages. The speed with which technology continues to evolve is ever increasing; even our telephone bill brings with it a new service each time - paging, call interruptions, and tracking the last caller! For children to develop as readers they need to experience the texts representative of the world outside the classroom.

Contrary to popular belief, the new technological age is not eliminating the need for literacy. Indeed, some aspects of it actually make new, more complex demands on our ability to read and write. The introduction of the Internet and e-mail are prime examples of the sophisticated nature of technological application of literacies required today.

Children have an entitlement to develop the knowledge, skills and understanding required by this technological society - indeed children are ahead of adults in terms of their knowledge of how certain computer packages work. Yet in classrooms, this media is often neglected; even the lone computer is rarely employed for 100 per cent of the school day. To say that children get enough technological exposure outside school is like saying that their understanding of geography can be left to rely upon the influence of the environment beyond the classroom.

In a curriculum which is already 'brimful and leaking' it is sometimes difficult to see where more can be squeezed in.

Information technology is, however, a clear strand which runs throughout the National Curriculum and IT practice can be seen at its best when applied purposefully within contexts across the curriculum. There is also a case for the inclusion of a more integrated language approach to the use of technology and other media in classrooms. The use of media technology for language learning can be powerfully effective, and the communication potential is rich. Computers provide many opportunities for reading, writing and discussion. There are many useful interactive learning software packages for spelling, grammar and punctuation. Games can provide the opportunity to read for meaning, particularly when instructions have to be followed. Communication skills are the very core of language. Writing, speaking, listening and reading can all be explored through these media, more often than not through models of learning which integrate the development of language skills within other curriculum areas.

This chapter presents a case for using media variety as a vehicle for developing children's reading. It is regarded as a complementary context for language work rather than an additional subject area. In other words, by turning to the mass media, teachers can tap into a gold seam of resources for relevant, effective and exciting work on all aspects of language.

MEDIA AND READING SKILLS

Reading is a complex activity involving a web of skills, knowledge and understanding. The chart below illustrates important reading skills which can be developed through the different media technologies. Each technology is then explored in greater depth with some reference to examples of classroom activities.

Medium	Reading Skills, Knowledge, Understanding	Examples of thematic content
newspapers	scanning skimming reading for meaning comparing fact and opinion bias	printing publishing editing interviewing current events
magazines	all of the skills above biography use of index cross-referencing page layout information retrieval multi perspective descriptions	subject areas, for example computers gender issues advertising
advertising	fonts/colours/graphics relationship between text and pictures motif and slogan inferential reading (reading between the lines) making connections responses	power of advertisement stereotypes fact and fiction economy of language
television	dramatic structure play scripts communication reviews critical analysis character discussion genre critical viewing making choices making comparisons character analysis script writing reviews news readers teamwork	viewing times surveys, for example favourite programmes subject areas, for example wildlife TV industry current affairs

NEWSPAPERS

Newspapers provide us with a wealth of reading material and back copies are free. There are different types of newspapers: Sunday; evening; daily; free; tabloid; broadsheet; national; local. They can all be used for a range of purposes, such as summarising, distinguishing between fact and opinion, comparison of reporting, matching headline to story, etc.

SORTING

It is a useful exercise to introduce children to the notion of choice and diversity.

Activity 1: Categories

Providing them with a large, representative selection of the variety of newspapers and asking them to sort them into categories will bring about much discussion and debate. The process will, inevitably, involve looking at style, layout, print type, ratio of text to photographs, size and pattern of publication, etc. There is an obvious overlap between some groups of newspapers: Sunday papers, for example, are also national. A cross-curricular link would be to ask the children to produce a Venn diagram showing their results.

LOCAL STORIES

Local newspapers can provide the best supply of interesting reading material in the classroom, particularly for younger children. The content will include stories to which they can relate because they are about the local area, and may even feature people they know. Local papers might be used as the starting point for many types of activity.

Activity 2: Reading for information

Look at the weddings page and make a list of all the churches and register offices to see which is the most popular location. This simple activity requires children to read for meaning, collect information of a specific nature and draw conclusions from that information. In addition, the fact that they are using 'grown-up' reading materials can be a valuable way of promoting children's self-esteem and perceptions of themselves as readers.

Activity 3: Filling out forms

Design a Police Report Form for the children to fill in using information from a crime story. You might include headings to complete such as:

- witnesses
- location of crime
- time of crime
- nature of crime
- victim's name
- victim's address.

There may be other headings which you could include on such a form depending on the material you use. The children should learn that sometimes, when filling out forms, it is acceptable to write 'not applicable' or 'not known'. This type of activity can be differentiated very easily by using different stories, designing simpler or more complex forms. The activity could be developed further by writing imaginary accounts from a witness with a different perspective, writing editorial opinion, or even re-writing the report in a different style. To engage with these writing activities, the pupils will need to read for meaning, select information (which will use scanning and skimming skills), interpret and evaluate information and read from an alternative prospective - all of which are valuable reading skills for the developing reader.

Most adults are aware of the political nature of newspapers, reflected by press ownership and bias in editing and reporting. Teachers must be wary when involving Junior children in political value judgements where the discussion is bound to involve the central beliefs of their home-life. It would, for instance, be inappropriate and unprofessional for a teacher to present a damning declaration on the morality of *The Sun* when it is quite possible that this is the only reading material the child ever encounters in their home. In the same way, it would be wrong to decry the right wing reporting of *The Sunday Telegraph* when children may be familiar with the paper and relate to its literacy and, indeed the politics, at home. It is irresponsible to believe that we can sway the political beliefs of our children. Not only is this abuse of our role, it is also giving damaging messages to children about the partnership between home and school. It is possible for teachers to recognise alternative literacies to their own and to be sensitive to the literacy experiences of the home without making value judgements.

It is, however, valuable to increase our children's critical skills without introducing bias of our own. Comparing reports of the same story in different newspapers can show children the differences in style and the selective presentation of information. Through carefully planned activities with appropriately selected material, children can be faced with decisions and form opinions of their own using the evidence before them. Examining fact versus opinion can be a useful way to encourage children to discriminate between what they read.

Activity 4: Comparing reports

Collect reports of the same story from four different newspapers. This is particularly interesting for pupils when a topical and up-to-date story is used. The children could use these reports for various activities including:
- discussing the different headlines of the same story;
- comparing the location and prominence of each version;
- measuring the space given to the reports;
- making an information grid to compare the facts stated in each report;
- looking up any new vocabulary;
- counting the number of sentences in each report;
- working out the average length of the sentences in each report;
- comparing reports for bias of opinion.

MAGAZINES

The publishing industry is currently enjoying a broad readership of a whole range of magazines. Their prominence in the child's world has also become more significant in recent years as sales outlets have increased to include petrol stations and supermarkets as well as traditional newsagents. The categories of magazines are even more numerous than for newspapers. One way to sort them could be as follows: men's; women's; children's; general; hobbies; compilations; information; quiz booklets; educational; professional; television guides.

Magazine formats can be a useful area of study. There are areas of commonality and also differences between the categories of publication listed above, and these can provide a useful framework for some activities in school.

Activity 1: Design and make a magazine

Sorting through and compiling the term's topic work so it can be pasted into a finished book is common practice in many schools. Provide additional learning by allowing the children to study magazine formats and design their books accordingly. Children could consider:

- use of a thematic index page;
- a variety of types of article;
- text size and layout;
- relevance of illustration;
- advertising;
- editorial comment;
- fact and fiction;
- cover design features.

Comparing magazines is a useful way to develop critical awareness. Impressionistic views can provide a starting point, but encouraging children to justify or explain a point by giving an example from the text will develop an important skill. Children's magazines and comics are an excellent resource because children can engage with these texts in an authoritative and motivated way.

Texts can be examined for bias, fact and fiction, stereotypes, and manipulation of information.

Reading for information is often associated with non-fiction and reference books in classrooms, yet magazines can provide a wealth of information, and opportunities to practise higher order reading skills. The TV guides are a particular rich seam of resources for activities of this nature. They can require scanning, skimming, cross-referencing, use of contents page, reading for information, fact, fiction, opinion, news and views. As an additional bonus, children usually love looking at them!

Activity 2: Sequencing TV programmes

The 'What's On This Week' pages at the front of guides usually have a scrap book of snippets from different programmes, often accompanied by photographs. Ask the children to cut these out individually then match them to the right day, time and channel for the programme. They could then sequence these into chronological order. Much more fun than a worksheet!

ADVERTISING

Half a term's work could be planned on the subject of advertising! The cross-curricular potential is obvious - tracing the growth of advertising (history), identifying and using the different forms of art work and graphic design (art and technology), fair testing of different products (science), examination of environmental issues (geography) to name but a few! The language work is implicit within the very purpose of advertising - communication. Language activities based on advertising are easy to differentiate due to the vast quantity of texts available at different levels of readability. At one end of the scale large slogans and captions could be used for phonic work, whilst at the other end, children could explore the metaphors and messages within those slogans and captions.

Activity starting points:

Discuss the pattern, shape and meaning of slogans.

Discuss the variety of styles of art work including photography.

Look at the blurb and ask the children to decide what audience is being targeted. How do they know?

How have the advertisers carefully planned this?

Allow the children to scan other magazines and newspapers and compare other adverts which have a clear selling pattern.

The children could then choose a known product from a selection and design an advertisement. They could employ the style of a real advert or employ some new techniques of their own.

A further extension could be to design their own products and selling campaign. This would provide a wealth of cross-curricular activities, particularly technology, in addition to an integrated language approach where speaking, listening, writing and reading would interrelate.

TELEVISION AND VIDEO

Television is a major influential force in children's lives. If a project on television is undertaken with Junior children, data handling work on hours of viewing will quickly demonstrate what a large proportion of hours is dedicated to viewing, particularly when compared with time spent in school, in bed, playing, and reading. This enthusiasm for television can be a helpful factor when planning to use it as a medium in classroom activities.

Critical and analytical awareness can be nurtured through use of video and television material, and much language work is appropriate within this context. Aspects relating specifically to reading development can be broadly divided into two categories:

1. evaluation and analysis of programmes
2. dramatisation/animation of literature

1. EVALUATION AND ANALYSIS OF PROGRAMMES

Television programmes can provide a familiar and comfortable context to explore the language of response, evaluation and critical analysis. Soap operas, for instance, have much to offer in terms of discussion. Why do the last 20 seconds of 'Neighbours', for example, always make you long for the next episode? How does this technique compare with the endings of chapters in stories? Why do many authors write in the same way? What about the authors who do not? What do you think of Character A in Soap B? Why do you think she did C? etc. Children should be encouraged to develop their own views and, most importantly, refer to actual examples to justify the points they make. In addition to building firm foundations for discussion and debate, using television in evaluative activities can also raise children's critical awareness and, perhaps, help them to become more discriminating in their viewing.

Developing children's confidence and competence in this way is likely to assist them when discussing texts in the same way.

2. DRAMATISATION/ANIMATION OF LITERATURE

There are many good dramatisations and animations of children's literature; for example 'Woof' by Alan Ahlberg, 'Goggle Eyes' by Anne Fine, 'The Railway Children' by E. Nesbitt, 'The Secret Garden' by F. Hodgson-Burnett and, of course, the BBC Shakespeare animations. Using such material in the classroom should not be regarded as a mere replacement for the text, rather it can be an enhancement. Discussion of dramatisations and adaptations can assist children to develop the language of critical analysis. It can help to build confidence in developing individual responses, expressing those responses and supporting views with referential evidence.

If the book is read first, children can discuss how characters in the film compare with their own imaginings. Closer examination of certain scenes can be compared with the book to identify adaptation and editing. The literal translation can be evaluated and also the way in which the book's inferential aspects have been exploited by the adaptation.

If the video is watched first, the children can be supported through more challenging texts, possibly reading extracts of books which they would otherwise not be ready for. Certain scenes can be viewed and then written in the style of the author. It is often noted by teachers that children, particularly reluctant readers, like to read the books of programmes and films. This motivating factor should be considered for children who need that extra stimulation.

COMPUTERS IN THE CLASSROOM

There are three important dimensions to the purpose of computers in the classroom.

There is the cross-curricular use of a range of software

which can provide information and skills relevant to different subject areas. Data handling, maths investigations, mapping databases, historical and scientific problem-solving, and music composition activities are amongst the most popular types of software. For schools that are able to afford CD-Rom multi-media machines, the sophisticated encyclopaedia programs now available can provide children with information for all areas of the curriculum, including sound and graphics in addition to texts.

Secondly, there is the use of hardware as part of the technology education entitlement to which all children should have access. How computers are managed and organised within the classrooms can convey messages to children about how they are regarded as users. By providing opportunities for children to use the hardware as part of their everyday business, teachers are making an important statement about the function of computers in society. This can make a significant contribution to how children perceive themselves functioning in that society. For instance, in classrooms where boys are nearly always chosen to set up the computer, girls are almost inevitably going to feel less confident about the way they are respected as competent users. Similarly, in classrooms where a 'turn' on the computer is offered only as a 'treat' when all the work is finished, children can be expected to regard computers as playthings rather than useful tools for their learning.

Thirdly, communication is a major function of the work which takes place at the computer. Language software can facilitate the development of literacy and oracy for children at all levels of ability. The talk which occurs between pairs of children working together at the computer can be the fruitful and constructive talk of discussion, planning, correcting, debating, informing, questioning, answering, decision-making and evaluation. Word processing programmes enable children to write in a variety of ways for different purposes, and are a particular asset for re-drafting and creative presentation of work. These modes are widely used in primary classrooms. It is the final mode - reading - which is, perhaps, underestimated as an appropriate learning activity to be scheduled for computer work. Early year classrooms employ software to enhance work in spelling, phonics and sentence construction. Many publishers now supply CD-Roms to supplement their reading schemes. The reading which children do to follow instructions in software for other areas of the curriculum is, of course, working in an integrated way to develop reading: reading for meaning in order to carry out a task interacting with screen texts in order to respond in a variety of ways. There is a tendency, however, to regard such activity as part of early reading development or support for special needs children.

Struggling readers over the age of seven might be given a task at the computer to develop their reading skills, but the tendency is to disregard the facility for other readers. So how can computers be used with the whole cross-section of the Junior ability range in order to contribute towards their reading development?

INTEREST AND PLEASURE

• Children's motivation is usually high when working on a computer.
• A wide range of texts can be used either discretely or for integrated work.
• The medium enhances other materials used.
• The interactive nature of computers sustains interest levels.

INDEPENDENCE

• Children can take responsibility for their own learning.
• Computers facilitate an independent work mode.
• Reading is part of the interactive process of computer activities.

SHARED READING

• Shared responses are actively stimulated by computer work.
• Discussion of texts can take many useful forms.
• Shared responsibility for reading computer texts can provide a peer support model.

INFORMATION RETRIEVAL

- Involves a range of strategies.
- Involves a range of materials (thesaurus, spell check, encyclopaedia, data bases, choice menus etc.).
- Fluency and accuracy are assisted by computer support devices.
- Organisation systems vary and provide good models.
- Active interrogation of texts is required, helping to develop questioning techniques and the development of clear research questions.

RANGE OF STRUCTURES

- Many formats are employed by computer programs.
- Different response features are required by those formats.

INTERACTIVE FICTION DEDUCTION

- Makes new and different demands on readers (for example activates story development based on deduction).
- Allows multi-dimensional reading (for example requires cross-checking).
- Gives the reader the power of control over texts.
- Encourages debate before decision-making.

EVALUATION

- Evaluations can be based on use and evidence.

LINKS WITH WRITING

- Word processing can provide additional contexts for readership (for example editing, proof reading, publishing, simulation of e-mail to send messages).
- Programs designed to develop skills such as spelling, phonics and use of contextual clues target specific reading operations.

RADIO AND TAPES

Sometimes regarded as the poor relation of television, radio is often forgotten in the classroom. The BBC schools' broadcast service offers a valuable range of programmes which can be used live or recorded. Included amongst many types of programmes are plays, stories, historic documentaries, poetry, discussions and debates. The National Curriculum requirements for English include a focus on children's listening skills and radio and tapes are obvious media for developing these. Many radio stations offer a resource which can be used as a stimulus for activities which relate to reading, for example, listening to news reports and comparing them with written reports in newspapers.

A large part of the work which can develop reading from using radio relates to scripts. Listening to radio plays, documentaries and discussion programmes can present a fine model for children's writing, and promote opportunities to look at different forms of writing, for example, comparing direct and indirect speech with script form. Making their own 'radio programmes' using cassette recorders can be an exciting challenge to children, and is a worthwhile vehicle for a range of language work.

Tapes, likewise, present learning opportunities. Many classrooms have listening corners. Older children enjoy listening to stories and the provision of a wide selection of talking books can serve them well in maintaining and developing their interest in literature. These are on loan at most public libraries, should school funds not stretch to their purchase. Selections range from Dick King-Smith to Jane Austen and therefore offer differentiated provision for this activity. Enabling children to make tapes for others to hear is another approach. They are far more likely to read with expression if they know that the reading is for a specific and public purpose.

THE COST OF MULTI-MEDIA RESOURCES

It is clear that there are many multi-media tools available to teachers which can be employed for continued development of Junior readers. The issue of cost has not been discussed so far, although it is certainly an important factor when considering and planning the provision of such resources in the classroom. It might be useful to consider the following questions when thinking about the financial implications of using a range of media in the classroom.

- Do we have any existing resources which are currently underused?
- Do we have a large investment in hardware which is wasted because the software is insufficient?
- Do we have a policy on the purchase of software, just as we do on the purchase of books?
- Is there more potential for sharing software?
- How can we ensure whole school progression in the use of software?
- Do all classes have adequate access to television?
- Are all radios and tape recorders in school used to their maximum potential?
- Can any parents come in to talk about how they use technology at work?
- Could communications/technology companies offer a visit or supply information packs?
- Are there opportunities for children to answer the school telephone or use the fax machine?
- What resources can we acquire which will cost us nothing? For example, used copies of newspapers, magazines and catalogues, unwanted telephones.

SUMMARY

The acknowledgement that multi-media can provide an invaluable range of resources to assist the development of Junior readers opens up a whole new world of ideas to creative teachers. With careful planning which addresses a clear understanding that the teaching of reading continues beyond the age of seven, different models of learning can be provided in Junior classrooms. Reading across the curriculum is part of the every day business of children's work. There is no doubt that the discrete teaching of reading also has an important part to play. The multi-media context is just one of the ways in which this can be managed effectively, with learning which is both effective and enjoyable as a feasible and self-evident outcome.

FURTHER READING

Bazalgette, C. (1991) *Media Education*, Hodder & Stoughton.

BFI Education (1989) *Primary Media Education: A Curriculum Statement*, British Film Institute.

Craggs, C. (1992) *Media Education in the Primary School*, Routledge.

Harpley, A. (1990) *Bright Ideas: Media Education*, Scholastic Ltd.

Walker, S. (1993) *Desktop Publishing for Teachers*, Reading and Language Information Centre, University of Reading.

Webster, C. (1992) 'The language of media' from *The Essential Guide to Language*, Folens.

Reading IT: A Teacher's Guide to the Use of Computers in Reading Activities, Reading and Language Information Centre, University of Reading.

CHAPTER 6

ASSESSMENT

In this chapter we will discuss various aspects of reading and classroom organisation, and how assessment opportunities can be part of the reading curriculum. The focus is on the formative nature of assessment: how assessment shapes planning and how teachers can assess the reading strands in the curriculum. In particular, we will address the involvement of the child in the assessment process and the knowledge required by the learner. We will also discuss the need for children both to understand and respond to what they have read; to use inference and deduction; to evaluate what they have read and to refer to the text to support opinions. This discussion is linked to the requirements of the National Curriculum and to recent research.

Valid assessment can occur only in an environment which is organised for learning. By developing group reading, discussion, and critical evaluation of texts and by involving children at all stages of the process, assessment becomes integral to the reading process and can lead to individual, summative statements which reflect planning, practice and future work. To begin with, it may be worth considering how and why reading tests have been used.

READING TESTS

Since 1960 the increase in standardised reading tests has been enormous. Local authorities, schools and teachers wanted some form of assessment that would indicate how their children were performing against national criteria. Reading tests which were seen as impersonal, reliable and quick to administer seemed the logical answer. With the introduction of the National Curriculum and the Standard Assessment Tasks and Tests at the end of Year 2 and Year 6, however, the place of other tests has been questioned.

Our understanding of the reading process and what it involves has increased considerably in recent years. It is important to bear in mind how we define reading before making any evaluation of reading tests. If your school is seriously considering spending money on a standardised test then, prior to reviewing or purchasing any reading tests, it would be well worth staff spending time in discussing how reading is taught throughout the school and in developing an agreed definition or description of reading. It will also be important for all staff to consider what it is that a reader knows and does in order to *read, understand* and *respond* to texts.

As our understanding of the reading process has been heightened, so we need to examine reading tests very closely to discover exactly which skills it purports to test and which skills it does *not* test. With this appreciation of the necessary skills and understandings, staff will be in a better position to make judgements about standardised reading tests. As part of the evaluating process, and in order to make judgements about the value of a standardised test, staff could discuss the following questions:

• Does it reflect their previously agreed description of a reader?
• Does it assess the knowledge, skills and understanding they have decided a reader needs?
• If it does not do either of the above then what does it do?

It is worth considering a few tests used in schools to help us to define terms.

STANDARDISED TESTS

Standardised tests are produced in a variety of formats, for example: single word, multiple choice, whole sentence and cloze passages. Some standardised tests have a diagnostic element. Before publication these tests will have been trialled and standardised on a large sample of children and a score developed from this.

Standardised tests fall into two broad categories – those that require the teacher to work with an individual child and those that can be administered to a group.

INDIVIDUAL TESTS

Single word tests

The *Schonell Reading Test* is an early example, it was first published in 1945 and is famous for its first line:

tree　　little　　milk　　egg　　book

These words increased in difficulty down the page and finally presented:

rescind　　metamorphosis　　somnambulist　　bibliography idiosyncrasy

The test culminated in the calculation of a 'reading age'. This was achieved by adding the number of words correctly read and using the formula:

$$RA = \frac{number\ of\ words\ read\ correctly}{10} + 5\ years$$

We might now rightly question the view that the five years addition was to take account of each child's first five years of identical experiences on this earth. Researchers into baseline assessment would not accept such a premise.

Nowadays, a reading quotient is obtained by taking the reading age (RA) and applying the following formula:

$$Reading\ Quotient = \frac{Reading\ Age\ X\ 100}{Chronological\ Age}$$

Thus a child with a reading age of 8y 6m and a chronological age of 8y 6m would achieve a Reading Quotient of 100. The view underpinning this is the notion of linear progression in relation to age and a score of 100 is the average for a specific age. The implication in our example above is that this reader is right on target! Where reading development is related to age, the premises that shape this calculation need to be challenged. It is certainly not helpful for a parent to be led to believe that these two ages should be parallel. Is it helpful to know a child's reading age based on such a test when it is clearly setting out to assess only one aspect of reading?

Graded sentence tests

This type of test consists of a series of unrelated sentences which are either read aloud or completed in writing:
The Holborn or *The Salford Sentence Reading Tests* are popular examples. A sentence from Holborn reads:

> Quench your thirst by drinking a glass of our sparkling ginger ale.

and a sentence for children achieving a reading age of 9.4 in the Salford Reading Test reads:

> Arthur's unusual and attractively shaped moustache certainly improves his appearance.

Once again, it is important to question the out-dated language and the mismatch between experience and reality on the one hand and the test on the other.

These graded sentence tests provide comparative data, in that the best readers can read and understand them, others can decode them but not understand and the strugglers can do neither. Recognising words in isolation or in decontextualised sentences is only a small part of reading and if it does not reflect how a child has been taught then it is not valuable. This form of testing is not concerned with a reader's understanding of a text, rather, value is placed only on the physical, voiced production of the words.

GROUP READING TESTS

These save on teacher time, in that they can be given to a large group simultaneously, are relatively easy to administer and some are designed to cover the whole primary age range. The easier something is to administer and mark, however, the less likely it is to give detailed information related to reading strategies.

Group tests vary considerably. Some are simple word recognition tests in which the pupil is offered a choice of words and is expected to circle the most likely one. For example, *Group Reading Test* (D. Young 1992). Some use cloze procedures which vary from single words deleted from a series of unrelated sentences (cloze reading tests) to others which provide a complete story (Word Search). More popular are those tests which provide a collection of different kinds of tests: word recognition, sentence completion, comprehension, reading rate and cloze procedure (*Edinburgh Reading Tests*). Some of the more recently published tests provide a reading booklet and a separate answer booklet. These are much closer in format to the assessment in the present Key Stage 2 SAT. The answer booklet requires some word recognition, but is more directed at literal and inferential interpretation (*Effective Reading Tests*, 1986).

Group reading tests appear to save time because they can be administered to large groups of children. They do, however, often take a long time to mark and the value of the information gained from these tests needs to be considered carefully. The children may have learned the skill of answering questions in a particular way, but has the teacher really learned anything new about the child as a reader?

DIAGNOSTIC TESTS

Since they require an oral reading, these tests generally enable teachers to observe how a child approaches the task. Reading aloud is, however, usually regarded as a performance read where the focus is on keeping a listener interested. Generally, prior to reading aloud, a reader will read the passage silently in order to understand what it means. Only then does he or she practise the use of voice, intonation and pace. If children are deprived of the opportunity to read to themselves and establish meaning before reading aloud, they are disadvantaged. They concentrate only on the production of the words. Thus any diagnostic assessment of understanding may be completely inaccurate.

A well known example of a test with a diagnostic element is the *Neale Analysis of Reading Ability*, originally published in 1958. It was revised in 1988 so that it no longer contains such sentences as:

> The milkman's horse had wandered in the fog.

The recently published *Diagnostic Reading Record* (H. Arnold

1992) sets out to assess reading, offering a graded set of passages to be read aloud using miscue analysis, and through discussion, a child's understanding of what has been read.

Miscue analysis is a procedure for analysing what children do when reading a text aloud. It involves observing, recording and evaluating strategies used by a reader. The procedure provides insights into how a reader reads, approaches unknown words, and if or how they attempt to correct words that have been misread. Information gained in this way enables the teacher to assess:

- whether the reader is aware of cueing strategies
- the reader's ability to draw on a range of cueing strategies
- whether there is an overdependence on one strategy

The procedure is based on the work of Kenneth and Yeta Goodman.

A final thought helps us to see how reading tests and the reading curriculum conflict. Good books for children contain a range of linguistic features including literary constructions, as well as spoken forms. By this we mean the use of adverbial phrases, non-finite clauses and subordinate clauses all of which are central to the rich use of language. These texts are in sharp contrast to the artificial language of so many schemes and tests. Hardly any of the tests we have examined contain such rich language. Examples in recent literature for children provide models of such structures:

> When he was not looking after Mowzer, he passed the day in the most useful way possible.
>
> Soothed by the sweetness of Mowzer's serenade, the Great Storm-Cat paused in his prowling and pulled back his giant cat's paw.

(from *The Mousehole Cat* by Antonia Barber and Dawn Bailey)

> Deaf now to the bewitching song, they sped down the hill, anxious not to lose sight of the witches.

(from *The Witches and the Singing Mice* by Jenny Nimmo)

Would it not be better to use such texts to both teach the skills of reading at Key Stage 2 and to make diagnostic assessments?

So why is it that teachers have been prepared to accept reading test results? It is because they *appear* to corroborate their own assessments. That is they identify the weak, middle and strong readers, but teachers know this before they administer the test. Most reading tests set out to assess only one aspect of reading. This they achieve, sometimes well and sometimes badly, but they do not and cannot cover other very important aspects of the skills of reading which include interest, enthusiasm, response and stamina.

TEACHING AND ASSESSMENT

In this section we are going to examine what we have come to mean by the use of the terms *understanding* and *response*, and we will also consider how *reading across the curriculum* can be assessed. It is our intention to make links between teaching and assessment and to show that well planned teacher assessment far exceeds the demands of any test we have looked at, and is also more informative.

Two principal elements of reading assessment are: whether the reader understands what is being read, and how the reader responds.

UNDERSTANDING

Understanding involves much more than old style comprehension. It embodies notions of:
• confidence in choosing, discussing, and summarising texts;
• appreciation of both the major points in a text, and its subtleties and ambiguities;
• familiarity with reference material and retrieval strategies.
The elements of readerly behaviour identified above indicate that a reader understands not only that reading should make sense, but also that meaning is created through interaction with the text. In working to understand the text, a reader is actively engaged in this process. This process in turn influences what kind of approach the reader adopts and thus the understanding and response are inter-dependent.

RESPONSE

Response is complex and difficult to describe. It involves the reader in:

• expressing opinions with references to the text;
• being prepared to adjust ideas in the light of reflection and discussion;
• being aware of themes and images;
• considering the structure of texts and how authors use language to achieve their effects.

You may wish to consider the following description of response in the light of your own reading and in relation to the planning for, and assessment of, the Key Skills for Reading at Key Stage 2. It is adapted from Teaching of Reading 2, produced by PAGE for Oxfordshire County Council (OCC, 1993) and is further described by H. Mitchell and J. Monk in a chapter of *The Primary Teacher's Guide to the New National Curriculum* (Ashcroft and Palacio, eds, 1995, Falmer Press).

> In assessing response we are looking to see that children
> move through the following stages, but not in a linear way.
> All language learning is recursive. Levels of attainment can
> only be a touchstone in this spiralling process. Movement
> within and along this spiral is only achieved in discussion
> with others.

INITIAL RESPONSE

• an immediate reaction to what has been read or heard;
• the reader may consider alone or with others and this may lead to an informal recommendation.

This can be achieved in the classroom through: oral book reviews, story swaps, top ten lists and so on. Information can be recorded in observational notes, log entries and through reading interviews.

CONSIDERED RESPONSE

• reflection on an initial response;
• the reader questions alone, or in discussion with others, what is suggested or hinted at in the text and/or illustration.

You will need to promote the discussion of: story openings,

scene setting, mood and character introduction; character actions and motives; story structure and plot development. Assessment can be made by tape-recording discussions and through observational notes.

RECONSIDERED RESPONSE

• a more conscious exploration of possible meanings;

• the reader thinks beyond the literal meaning to what is implied;

• the reader may make associations with past experiences or previous reading.

You will need to draw attention to inferential meanings within a text. That is to say those meanings that are not made explicit in the text. They are implied by the writer for the reader to detect and draw on as meaning is shaped and responded to. Consideration of a character's actions or conversations provide opportunities to explore what is implied and what might be inferred. Comparisons can be made between different tellings of folk and classic tales in traditional and modern settings, for example, Arthurian Legends, or *The Odyssey*. Such work will help to develop inferential reading.

Assessment can be through discussion, reading interviews or an in-depth review with question prompts.

CRITICAL RESPONSE

• by challenging and questioning the values embedded in the text, the reader questions the author's intentions and is required to make a viewpoint explicit to others.

Your children will need time to discuss and compare texts; to make links across a range of texts; to reflect on initial impressions of their reading to justify their opinions with reference to details in the text and/or illustrations, and to consider thematic links, such as, bravery, jealousy, a view of the future. An excellent framework for booktalk can be found in *Tell Me* (Chambers, 1993).

READING ACROSS THE CURRICULUM

Traditionally, children's reading has been assessed in the

context of fiction. As teachers we are aware that a skilled reader needs many other competencies. For example: the ability to read selectively; locate information swiftly and accurately; be fully aware of the purposes for reading.

When faced with a text on a subject about which we know little, we become novice readers once more. Every kind of reading requires different reading strategies. The Programmes of Study identify this and outline a comprehensive list of strategies required to read and learn from non-fiction texts. The difficulty in school with regard to this issue is that, as a rule, children learn to read through fiction and they experience difficulty in adjusting their reading behaviour to non-fiction texts. The work of Littlefair (1991), Mallett (1992) and Neate (1992) has begun to outline some of the challenges and solutions. Children need a clear purpose and a structured opportunity to extract and absorb information and to use it purposefully for a known outcome, (PAGE–OCC, 1994).

A useful way to assess a child's stage of development in reading non-fiction, might involve looking at the degree to which he or she understands and uses the following:

- text organisation and page layout including headings, fonts, format, print style;
- contents, indexes and glossaries;
- diagrams, drawings, photographs etc.;
- reference material including encyclopaedias, dictionaries, and thesauruses;
- different ways of representing the information obtained;
- the techniques of:

a) skimming a page to gain an overall impression

b) scanning to locate information

c) detailed reading for specific information.

National Curriculum Key Stage 2 Reading, para. 2c.

There are many other suggestions in the work of Neate (1991) and Mallett (1992) and new developments can be found in the work of Lewis and Wray with the EXEL Project, (Primary Professional Bookshelf 1995).

STANDARD ENGLISH AND LANGUAGE STUDY

Teacher assessment of Standard English and language study can be managed in several ways during regular classroom activities. Here the teacher is concerned to assess how the reader uses the following:

• the language and features of different texts (for example narrative, information, description, argument);

• comparisons of texts to show how authors exploit the features of a genre creatively;

• awareness of the author's use of language and the intended impact on the reader;

• appropriate vocabulary to discuss reading (for example introductory statement, sub-heading, phrase, chapter, plot);

• an awareness of how language varies and changes over time;

• knowledge of word derivation, root words and loan words to aid understanding.

Notes of a child's growing competence can be made by observing individual or group research reading, observing booktalk, through brief conversations during classroom activities or through the formal reading interview.

ASSESSMENT THROUGH OBSERVATION AND WAYS OF RECORDING

This section contains practical suggestions for use in school to observe, record and assess reading. It will show how such assessments can inform planning and subsequently lead to individual reading interviews. This section includes advice on:

• valid assessment

• assessment procedures including: observational notes
group assessments
individual assessments.

WHAT MAKES VALID ASSESSMENT?

Assessment is only valid if it:

• provides information about a child's development, including knowledge, skills and understanding;

- indicates the approaches and strategies a child uses for learning;
- provides evidence of achievement;
- informs planning and includes some specific notes for further teaching;
- encourages the child to reflect on him or herself as a learner.

WHO SHOULD BE INVOLVED?

All those who have a legitimate interest in the child, including:
- the teacher
- the child
- any other teacher or adult working with the child
- the parent or carer.

In this section we will describe a range of procedures adopted by teachers to monitor the progress of their children's reading. These will be discussed in terms of what is realistic and useful, and also takes account of what is possible. It must be acknowledged that some monitoring procedures are easy to manage but do not inform planning, neither do they provide evidence of strengths and weaknesses.

DEVELOPING ASSESSMENT PROCEDURES

Continuity, both in assessment and record-keeping procedures, is essential if cumulative data is to be accurate. If a school does not devise and agree a system to collect and pass on information to staff and parents, confusion will arise. Any inconsistencies will undermine all the efforts to compile a coherent profile of a child's language development. It is essential that, whatever systems are set up, all those responsible for their management agree on:
- the style and format of assessment and recording procedures
- the frequency with which they are carried out.

Once agreement has been reached, the main elements of classroom based, teacher assessment can be developed. These will be influenced by the assessment opportunities offered or identified in the schools scheme of work or curriculum development plan.

The very nature of teaching requires continuous assessment. A teacher in the classroom makes judgements about an individual child's achievements and needs throughout the day. The contributions that these observations make to a teacher's knowledge of a child should not be underestimated, but neither should it be necessary to record each observation. Teachers need to balance their judgements and decide which observations are significant and need to be recorded. The word *significant* is the key.

Considerations of how best to gather useful data should take account of the need for:

OBSERVATIONAL NOTES OF SIGNIFICANT DETAILS

This information can be gathered in the course of routine classroom activities, for example, by making notes during a group or class discussion or booktalk activity.

PLANNED, SYSTEMATIC RECORDING OF INFORMATION

Systematic recording requires the teacher to allocate a regular time to assessing an element of language development.

It is worth reminding ourselves of the advice in The Dearing Report (1993):

> Most primary schools keep detailed cumulative **reading** records. If these relate to the children's developing achievements in reading and are regularly updated, there is no need to keep any further records. Records of the title of the book being read and the date will not, however, be sufficient.
>
> (DES 1993, page 103)

ASSESSING READING – OVERALL CONSIDERATIONS

Fundamental to any form of assessment is the understanding of the reading process and what it involves. Readers use several cueing systems simultaneously and automatically. The reading process is a synthesis of close cues. They are often described under the following headings: **semantic knowledge, syntactic knowledge, and phonological knowledge and word recognition.**

SEMANTIC KNOWLEDGE

- the use of life experience to try to interpret what is happening and to predict what is about the happen;
- the use of immediate and previous textual context, including illustrations to help work out meaning.

SYNTACTIC KNOWLEDGE

- drawing on the patterns of spoken and written language to predict possible combinations of words and phrases;
- drawing on our experience of literary language to predict possible outcomes.

PHONOLOGICAL KNOWLEDGE AND WORD RECOGNITION

- checking symbol/sound associations when necessary, recognising some familiar words and parts of words.

English in the National Curriculum (1995) identifies key skills that readers need. These key skills relate very closely to the above description of the reading process.

They include:

- increased ability to read with fluency, accuracy, understanding and enjoyment;
- consideration of the quality and depth of what is read;
- response to plot, characters and ideas;
- use and knowledge of vocabulary and language structures;
- use of inference and deduction.

WHAT SUPPORTS TEACHER ASSESSMENT?

- A planned curriculum that allows for observation and recording.
- A clear view of what is being assessed.
- A recognition that teacher assessment will provide valid information.
- An agreed format.
- The use of a language for recording that is concise, accurate and understood by everyone involved.
- A knowledge of the range, key skills and language study elements in the curriculum.
- An appreciation of the inter-relatedness of speaking and listening, reading and writing.

On many occasions two of these elements can be assessed and recorded simultaneously.

OBSERVATIONAL NOTES

Opportunities to make observational notes occur all the time. Managing to commit observations to paper presents a challenge, but these observations are potentially a rich source of evidence. If all adults involved in the classroom recognise the value of jotting down their observations, it is possible to get a wider view of the child, in a range of group and learning situations that are not provided for in the planned assessment situation. Observational notes might refer to:

• significant contributions to a group discussion;
• observations made by the child indicating that he or she is making links with other experiences;
• a child's growing ability to work appropriately, deciding whether the task requires collaboration or independence.

Some teachers have found the following strategies useful:
• a working notebook carried in a pocket (or around the neck!)
• a card index
• a reading record book
• focusing on four children per day for brief periods.

GROUP AND INDIVIDUAL ASSESSMENT

These assessments should not be contrived. In every classroom, as part of the reading curriculum, there should be an expectation that books are discussed. Where such activities are not integral to practice, it is unwise to set up artificial situations and to expect children to discuss books in a meaningful way. In a classroom where the variety of reading activities includes groups of children regularly reading together from a range of texts, then assessment through discussion becomes normal practice. It is worth bearing in mind that group assessment allows for a different focus and the following chart indicates some of the differences between group and individual assessments.

Group assessment	Individual assessment
Semi-structured	Structured
Allows for points to be discussed and issues raised	Confirms level of understanding and response
Allows for response to plot, character, ideas and vocabulary	Can focus on a particular aspect in depth
Generally peer-group led and therefore less restricted	Always adult-led and needs to take account of child's starting point and level of confidence

GROUP ASSESSMENT

'Booktalk', a group discussion around a shared text, could provide evidence of the ability to read aloud, contribute to a discussion, build on the comments of others, pose pertinent questions, read beyond the literal, make links with other reading and support opinions by referring to the text. Thus assessment can be central to an activity.

An interesting study carried out by Sarah Oldham, a Year 4 B.Ed student, describes a structured approach to booktalk involving pair and group work, discussion of illustrations and questions that puzzled them over a period of five sessions. The group of eight-year-olds with whom she worked made comments that reflect progression which both can identify and the teacher can use for future planning:

In their first session they were asked: 'What do you talk about when you talk about books?'

In their first session, they responded as follows:
- Talk about likes and dislikes
- Name the book and its author
- Tell others what their book was about
- Talk about the title page
- Re-tell the story in their own words
- Talk about the 'blurb' on the back of the book
- Ask others their opinions about the book

READING: GROUP ASSESSMENT	Date: June 1995

Group Members
Vikki, Kizzie, Carl, Ian, Lauren, Gemma

Activity
Booktalk

Book Title, Author, Genre
Outside Over There, M. Sendak, Fantasy P/bk.

Strategies & Skills
Response – personal, critical; Knowledge about Language; Study Skills

All
• used pictures to infer meaning, for example mother's sadness, lack of interest.
• used text – read beyond the words – father's absence discussed at length.
• supported opinion with reference to the text.
• explored ideas, questioned, speculated – for example changing scene outside window – what might it mean?
• identified possible themes, for example Do as you're told, we should look after children.
   Ian:V. perceptive remarks about responsibility
   Vikki: made links with own experience caring for younger brother
   S/L: Speculation, building on contributors of others, listening attentively, summarising

Summary of Development/Forward Planning
• draw attention to relationship between text and pictures
- explore written and pictorial metaphor/symbolism
• discuss themes - provide range of texts
• compare Sendak's work
• consider how other characters may tell same story

- Discuss the pictures
- Talk about their views of the book and any disagreements.
  In session six they added the following:
- Talk about the layout of a book
- Discuss things that they do not understand
- Discuss colours and illustrations
- Discuss complicated pictures
- Discuss the meaning of difficult words
- Discuss alternative titles
- Discuss any puzzles or questions that arise from the reading of it.

The teacher's role in structuring discussion to ensure progression is central. By having clear teaching and learning objectives, it is possible to create assessment opportunities.

INDIVIDUAL ASSESSMENTS

A READING INTERVIEW

A reading interview provides a variety of information. For example, it can give insights into range and preference, author knowledge and knowledge about language. It does take time to do and can, realistically, be managed perhaps no more than twice in any one year. In schools where reading interviews are well established, children take much of the responsibility for deciding upon the focus and preparing for the interview.

The following section describes how to prepare for a reading interview and offers suggestions for conducting and recording the interview.

Preparation

Before embarking on a reading interview you will need to look through and review the child's reading record. In this way, you gain information about the child's range of reading and have an ideal starting point for discussion. This detailed outline covers the entire range of reading at Key Stage 2 and clearly you will not be carrying out the entire assessment at one time.

A reading review should be part of continuous assessment. In preparation for any reading review, posters (such as the one

WHAT'S IT ALL ABOUT?
• When reading your book, can you determine how the plot unfolds?
At what points in the story does the action speed up or the mood change?
• Choose a character...
What sort of person is he/she?
What part does he/she play in the story?
How does he/she behave towards other people?
• When you have finished your

shown left) could be made suggesting to the children some of the questions you will be asking. As well as asking individuals to refer to the poster, provide further questions for them to discuss during a group reading session. For example:

Choose a favourite book and consider the following:

• How does the plot unfold? At what points in the story does the action speed up or the mood change?

• Choose a character and describe their personality, their part in the story, their behaviour towards other people.

• What is the writer talking to us about in this book? That is, what are the themes and issues in the book?

• Choose a particularly memorable part of the book and comment on its effectiveness, selecting words, phrases and sentences, and explaining how the language achieves its effects.

• Does it remind you of any other stories, books or films?

Conducting the interview

Some teachers review all reading since the last interview, others make clear that the interview will have specific focus, for example, non-fiction or poetry. It may be helpful to arrange a time to discuss a particular aspect of reading, such as fiction or non-fiction. Ensure that the child brings any relevant books to the interview that he or she wants to refer to, for example, those books recently read individually or those read and discussed in a group or in the class. Whatever is being assessed, *it is important that the child is aware of what the focus of the discussion will be.*

Looking at range

Fiction and poetry:

This part of the interview should provide information on:

• the range of fiction and/or poetry read recently;

• personal reading preferences; the child should give clear reasons beyond simple likes and dislikes;

• the child's knowledge of several authors, and awareness of different writing styles;

• the child's understanding and ability to describe the differences between stories and poems, using appropriate vocabulary for example, 'character', 'chapter', 'rhyme', 'verse'.

Non-fiction:

Discussion of non-fiction as part of a reading interview is less common. Apart from reviewing non-fiction reading undertaken and why, this interview can provide insights into how the child finds his or her way round the books, and reads them, since the strategies for reading non-fiction are different from those required for reading fiction. Readers learn to disregard, re-read and use text organisation to help them locate and read specific parts of a text. Use a reference book or other information text, (for example chart, pamphlet, encyclopaedia) or invite the child to select from an existing collection.

• Ask the child how she/he would locate information on a topic covered by the book.

• With the child, select a page that has various features and discuss how to locate specific information quickly.

The discussion should provide information on understanding and awareness of:

• content, how the book is organised and the ability to use organisational devices to select and use information;

• the reader's ability to infer, deduce and draw on other knowledge and previous experience;

> READING NON-FICTION
> 1. Choose a non-fiction book.
> • Is there a table of contents?
> • Is there an index?
> 2. Turn to any page.
> • How is the page organised?
> • Are different fonts used?
> ~~~ and what ~~~

• purposes for reading (for example preference, motivation, specific purpose);

• how a writer's knowledge, experience and bias may influence a text.

Other reading including: brochures, playscripts, journals, magazines, advertisements:

This part of the interview establishes the wider range of reading the child may have undertaken. Frequently children feel that the reading they do outside school does not 'count'. Asking them to think about this area of their reading, not only makes clear to them that reading is much wider than that which takes place in school, but provides useful insight for the teacher into a child's reading habits and preferences.

• Discuss format, similarities, differences with other reading material.

• Ask the child whether any of the information is true, useful, or misleading; ask why he or she formed these opinions.

Long established literature:

If the child's reading record shows evidence of books in this category:

• Discuss with the child what 'long established' means to him or her.

• Explore his or her reasons for the choice.

• Read a passage together (or independently), or ask the child to select a piece known/liked/remembered and encourage reflection on language; consider how the same piece would be written today.

Remember that the aim of the interview is to build up a detailed picture of a reader over time and to provide useful information for both you and the child. It is impossible to focus on all these elements during one interview. The following questions have been included to help you conduct the interview.

RANGE AND PREFERENCE

Questions

- What books have you read recently?
- Are these all the same kind of books?
- What sort of books do you like to read?
- What kind of writing (genre) do you like reading best?
- Which authors/illustrators do you like best?

Evidence

To what extent can the reader describe the features of different books using appropriate vocabulary? (For example 'character', 'description', 'plot', 'chapter', 'verse', 'rhyme', 'rhythm', 'sub-headings', 'glossary', 'index'.)

Progress is measured through an increasing ability to express and explain preference (that is, more than simply 'I like it' or 'I don't like it').

EXPRESSING OPINIONS AND SUPPORTING VIEWS

Questions

Ask the child to select a passage he or she would like to discuss and then ask:

- Why did you choose this passage?
- What interests you about it?
- Have you read anything like this before?
- What did the writer want you to think about when you read this book?
- Which parts of the book tell you this?

Discuss the characters with the child and ask:

What was —'s role in the story?

Do you know anybody like —?

Evidence

Can the reader support his or her personal views by reference to details in the text.

Can the reader relate and compare texts and make thematic links.

Can the reader give reasons for his or her opinions on character, relating their answers to the text and to their own experiences.

READING NON-FICTION

Questions

- What non-fiction have you used recently?
- Do you prefer reading fiction or non-fiction?

Ask the child to choose a non-fiction book and then ask:

- How is this book organised? Why is this part in italics?

What is this (a key or an index) for?

Evidence

To what extent are the conventions of non-fiction texts used and explained?

Does the child use strategies appropriate for reading non-fiction? For example:

'I look at the whole page first and the illustrations, and then I scan the page for a particular word (Columbus, tectonic plates) which may be in bold. Then I read around it..., I look for headings.'

These questions are taken from the Oxfordshire Reading Record (1995).

CHILDREN ASSESSING THEIR OWN READING

As learners we are aware that knowing what we are trying to do and evaluating what we have achieved, can improve our efforts. This technique, if used in the classroom, helps children to understand what they are trying to achieve and allows them to contribute to any assessments made of their reading. The Cox Report (1989) highlighted the importance of making clear to children just what they are required to do.

> Self-assessment by pupils themselves, even at the Primary stage, has a part to play by encouraging a clear understanding of what is expected of them, motivation to reach it, a sense of pride and positive achievements and a realistic appraisal of weaknesses that need to be tackled. It should be given due weight as part of the evidence towards teachers' internal assessments.
>
> (DES, 1989, para 14:16)

Children will develop skills of reflection and self-assessment if they work in a classroom where the learning objectives are clearly identified, discussed and reviewed with them. These skills of self-assessment will be developed most successfully when children feel secure in being able to acknowledge areas of difficulty as well as success. The classroom activities we have described in this chapter, can all involve children in making judgements about themselves.

These activities do not need to take extra time; they can be part of regular reading routines. Some teachers have found that an effective way to develop children's self-assessments is through directed, specific discussion and recording activities. Ask children, for example, prior to a group or silent reading session, to notice particularly memorable phrases or think about a particular character. Following the reading session, any thoughts or comments can be discussed or jotted down in their reading logs. If children are shown *how* and *what* to record and if classroom time is made available for this process, assessment procedures will be very effective.

The following extracts from the Oxfordshire Reading Record Pupils Diary are intended to help children become effectively self critical and provide information for teaching and assessment.

Notes
Often when we read, we come across a specific word, phrase or way of saying something that we particularly like, or that we might be able to use ourselves in the future. This is *not* cheating. It can be very useful; all writers learn from other people.
useful, or memorable words and phrases

Forward planning:
books I intend to read and why
It is useful to have somewhere to jot down any books that you think you might like to read in the future. Your reasons for wanting to read them will be many and various, so make a brief note. For example: *I like this author; My friend thought it was good; I've seen the film/TV programme; Recommended by teacher; The cover looks exciting.*
Title   Reason

Forward planning: I need to...
In the classroom and probably at home too, or in conversation with friends, you may realise that you never read certain types of books, or that you know very little about a particular subject. Make notes here of things you think you should know more about. For example: *...read some science fiction; ...read some poetry; ...read books by different authors* (if you only read books by one particular author); *...know more about other religions; ...read more newspapers/know more about current events.*
I need to...

From: Oxfordshire Reading Record, Pupil's Diary, P.A.G.E. (Primary Advisory Group for English) 1994

MISCUE ANALYSIS/ RUNNING RECORD

Miscue analysis, running records and informal reading inventories are three of the terms used to describe methods of diagnostic assessment that focus on the strategies and reading competencies of individual children. *The Primary Language Record* (CLPE, 1988) advocates the use of this form of assessment, is described in the work of Arnold (1982) and Bielby (1994), and is reflected in the SATs for Key Stages 1 and 2.

The following example provides clear evidence of the value of such assessments. The reader is a Year 6 pupil considered by his teacher to be reading at Level 2. A key to the coding symbols used appears opposite.

Football Crazy Colin McNaughton

/ / / / /
Bruno was crazy about football.

/ / / / / *just nodded* / / / / / /
The trouble was, he had nobody to play with. He had just

/ / / / / / / / / / *sc* / / /
moved to the big city with his mum and dad (and) he didn't have

/ /
any friends.

/ / *T* / / / / / / / / /
It was Sunday, and he stood at the window and watched a

/ / / / *one* / / /
gang of kids playing on some waste ground.

/ / / / / / / / /
The gang called themselves Tex's Tigers. Bruno thought they

/ /
were terrific.

/ / / / / / / / / / / / /
He watched Tex flick the ball to Patch and Patch nod it over

/ / / / / / / / / / /
to Ginger and Ginger back (heel) it up to Roberto and Roberto

RUNNING RECORD PASSAGE–CODING SYMBOLS

correct reading   /   above every word read correctly

omission   (and)   circle word omitted

prompt   *T*   above any word that is told

substitution   *kept* / crept   write substitute above the correct word

phonics   *o·c·a·n* / ocean   write the sounds produced above the word

self correction   crept*(sc)*   write by word when self corrected (without help)

Other symbols that may be useful when analysing how a child reads:

insertion   /   '... and then / *he* found...'

hesitation   //   separate words with slashes for a hesitation of more than one second

repetition   <u>crept</u>   underline repeated word(s)

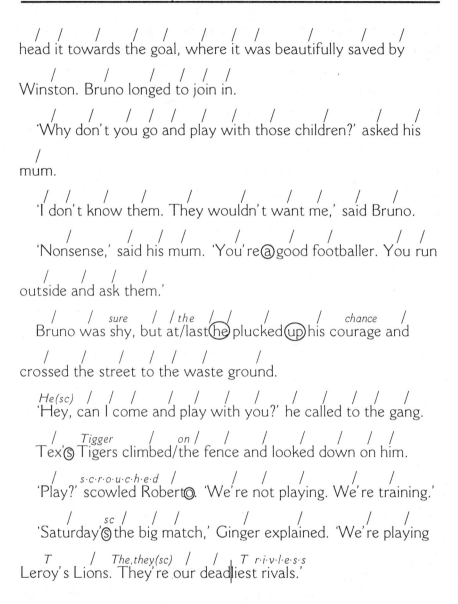

head it towards the goal, where it was beautifully saved by

Winston. Bruno longed to join in.

'Why don't you go and play with those children?' asked his mum.

'I don't know them. They wouldn't want me,' said Bruno.

'Nonsense,' said his mum. 'You're @ good footballer. You run outside and ask them.'

Bruno was shy, but at/last *he* plucked *up* his courage and crossed the street to the waste ground.

He(sc) 'Hey, can I come and play with you?' he called to the gang.

Tex *Tigger* Tigers climbed/*on* the fence and looked down on him.

'Play?' scowled Robert *s·c·r·o·u·c·h·e·d*. 'We're not playing. We're training.'

'Saturday's the big match,' Ginger explained. 'We're playing

T Leroy's Lions. They're our dead|iest *The,they(sc)* rivals. *T r·i·v·l·e·s·s*'

By marking the text that Jamie read, it is possible to analyse the cueing systems he uses to help him read aloud. We can see that, on the whole, Jamie is understanding what he is reading as he self-corrects several of his miscues. Where he is uncertain of the meaning, or encounters what appears to be an unfamiliar word, he uses phonic strategies, for example, 'scowled' 'rivals', and 'begged'. He also approximates, perhaps from other sources (for example, 'Tiggers'). In other places, he draws on linguistic knowledge and familiar language patterns to help him make sense of the passage. For example, he omits the 'o' at the end of Roberto, insets 'on' in climbed the fence and alters 'you' to 'he' in 'let's see what you can do?'.

It can be seen that Jamie draws on a range of strategies when he reads. When he was asked about his strategies for reading unknown words, Jamie's first reply was, 'I break words up and if I can't get them then, I sound them out.' He had to be prompted to describe how he read on and back in order to manage his self-corrections.

This assessment seems to indicate that, on the whole, what he seems to need now is more experience of the language of books and opportunities to hear and read well-written language regularly. A further conclusion to draw from this miscue, and the subsequent discussion with Jamie is that, for both teaching and learning, it is essential for us to help children make explicit to themselves all the skills that are synchronised in the process of reading.

There is some very helpful guidance in the SCAA publication, Exemplification of Standards (1995). It explains that progression in reading has to be considered in three broad areas:
• reading increasingly demanding texts using a repertoire of strategies;
• response to texts, including analysing and evaluating;
• reading for information.

Each of the case studies contains detailed information on the child's reading and writing and provides data on which judgements are made and further work considered.

ASSESSMENT AT THE END OF KEY STAGE 2

In this section we look at developments on the national scene and reflect on the futility of teaching to the tests or, worse still, practising the tests as a way to improve *scores* rather than *reading*.

From 1995 teachers agreed to carry out national assessment procedures at the end of Key Stage 2. The implications of this decision are far reaching in that the tests were, for 1995, marked externally, thus relieving teachers of the marking but at the same time shifting control and ownership elsewhere. Inevitably there have been complaints about marking procedures, cheating and unfair advantage. It is unusual, however, to read comments from teachers about the validity of tests that assess reading through writing.

In earlier pilots, reading interviews were trialled and dismissed by teachers as time consuming and yet, from the evidence already presented in this chapter, it would appear that such methods of assessment yield far more useful information.

SO WHAT DO THE SATS ASSESS?

Within the framework of the original National Curriculum for English (1989), it was necessary for the test developers to ensure that each strand of each Statement of Attainment was included in some way. It was therefore possible and indeed required, that the questions could be mapped on to the Statement of Attainment grid. Thus if a test was covering 4 levels then some 25–30 statements had to be covered. Indeed, in the Guidance for the 1994 pilot, the answer key indicates which statements are being assessed by each question. Thankfully, with the new Curriculum, we can now look forward to a less formulaic approach, but the level descriptions, nevertheless, have elements which will have to be assessed.

The guidance for teachers set out for the 1994 and 1995 Tests holds the key to practice.

> 'Children who are to be entered for the Level 3-6 Main
> Test should have experience of the following:
> • reading an increasingly wide range of texts, including fiction, non-fiction and poetry;
> • developing and expressing personal taste;
> • talking and writing about plot character and ideas in fiction;
> • referring to relevant passages or episodes to support their responses;

• reading different texts in different ways, such as skimming and scanning for information in non-fiction;

• finding information from other sources, such as databases, tables of contents, indexes and other tabular material.'

(SCAA 1994)

If you cannot show that a child is confident in these skills, then he or she should not be entered for that test.

In 1996 Level 6 will be assessed separately in recognition of the fact that it has proved to be almost impossible to write questions that will challenge the experienced reader sufficiently and, at the same time, not daunt the newly independent reader. Thus children entered for the higher level will need to focus on detail of plot, character and action in order to make judgements, predictions and draw conclusions. They will also be confident at distinguishing fact from opinion and appreciate use of language, vocabulary choices, metaphor and simile. They will be prolific readers of a wide range of material.

As we discussed in the section on reading tests, it is difficult to devise a test that meets the needs of a wide range of achievement. In order to deal with the range of reading competence reflected in the range from Level 3 to Level 5 or, as in 1994 and 1995, Levels 3–6, the questions in a SAT are devised using differentiation both through questioning and through outcomes. At the same time, they are attempting to cover all the aspects of the Programmes of Study with regard to range, key skills and standard English and language study. Cloze questions, such as the multiple choice questions, for the most part, assess literal understanding but the final questions in the section often explore inferential understanding. The level of understanding and detail in a written response is used to award a scale of marks for one question. No amount of practice at *doing* the tests, therefore, will help to move a child beyond Level 3. Inferential understanding is developed through discussion and reflection.

The SATs are, therefore, summative assessments and can

only indicate a child's level of achievement at that point in time. We may be able to make some formative judgements but these will not be conclusive, and can only be considered in conjunction with ongoing teacher assessment. General conclusions and trends can be highlighted and the report to schools on the 1995 tests will provide more in-depth error analysis than previously.

LEVELS 1–2

It has been worrying to see children who cannot be described as 'independent readers' being entered for the Level 3–6 test and then falling off the bottom of the scale and being awarded Level 2. There is little point in doing this, particularly as these are the very children who need a more detailed diagnostic assessment of their reading. It is also quite unnecessary when the Level 1–2 SAT at Key Stage 2 is so clearly designed to act as a diagnostic framework that will inform planning.

The guidance states quite clearly that children who are at the **stage of supported reading** should be entered for the Levels 1–2 Test. This will involve the selection of a book from a given list and the teacher should carry out a reading interview during which, children working within Level 2, will be assessed using a running record. This will take account of the strategies a child is or is not using and will assist the teacher in making an informed judgement. This approach is also being introduced in a modified form, at the end of Key Stage 3. It would be appear to be more satisfactory if running records or miscue analysis were being used throughout the primary school to provide a basis for diagnostic assessment and planning.

It is important for Key Stage 2 teachers to recognise that to achieve Level 2, a child is reading with 90 to 100 per cent accuracy from the selected text. Children who achieve Level 2 at the end of Key Stage 1 will begin Key Stage 2 with a SAT result which reflects the following range.

For national assessment purposes and for reporting to parents, children are given a reading grade of 2a, b or c. Judgement s are made about a child's ability to read with accuracy, fluency and understanding and how they understand and respond to what has been read. This information, from the KS1 SAT, coupled with teacher assessment, will provide useful data for the teacher of Year 3 children.

Accuracy, fluency and understanding

2c: at the earliest point of entry to Level 2 (i.e. 2c) a child reads with 90 per cent accuracy from a selected text, using some appropriate strategies and some inappropriate strategies and pauses to comment or confirm meaning.

2b: at 2b, the child's reading will be almost entirely accurate and well paced taking some account of punctuation. He or she is able to read ahead. The child sometimes noticeswhen the reading does not make sense, for example by self-correcting or making an attempt to resolve the problem, even if an unhelpful strategy is repeated.

2a: at 2a, the reading of the passage is accurate and the child tackles unfamiliar words with encouragement only. The child notices when the reading did not make sense, and takes appropriate action, for example self-corrects, looks back/forward in the text, or asks for meaning. The pace and fluency of the child's independent reading shows confidence, an ability to read ahead and the use of expression and intonation to enhance meaning.

Understanding and response

These will also be taken into account when deciding a grade.

At 2c the child comments on obvious characteristics, for example able to recognise good/bad characters (Angel/Wolf). Retellings of the story may be too short, too long and heavily reliant on illustrations.

At 2b the child comments on setting and how the plot is linked together or contains surprises. Reference to some features of presentation. Re-telling refers to most of the main events and characters. Is more likely to recall shared passage than passage read alone.

In order to achieve 2a, the child is able to identify and comment on main characters and how they relate to one another. Able to consider possible alternatives to events and actions. Re-telling is balanced and clear. Can comment on ways in which the story was presented.

(SCAA, 1995) Level 2: descriptions of a range of performance.

There are also case studies within this documentation that illustrate both achievement and ways forward.

For children working within Level 1 and Pre-Level 1, it is essential to recognise and to note the following:

- whether the child consistently recognises some words;
- the phonic strategies the child is using to read words in context;
- whether the child is keeping an overall sense of the passage in mind, for example by substituting a word that makes sense or being aware of language patterns;
- whether the child shows an awareness of punctuation, for example by pausing at appropriate places;
- whether the child is responding to what he or she is reading, either through comments, for example 'That Lumpty's house, he'll fall if he climbs up' or through laughter or gesture.
- whether the child follows the text accurately, for example by pointing or by knowing when to turn the page;
- whether the child is using knowledge of rhyme where appropriate.

(SCAA 1995) KS1 English tasks 1996. Reading and Writing Teacher's Handbook.

In reviewing this information the teacher should decide whether the child has shown sufficient independence to be awarded Level 1 based on the level description and the Programme of Study and whether the child should be considered for Level 2 assessment. If the child is not recognising enough words to sustain some momentum in a short passage then he or she should be considered as not yet achieving Level 1. Sadly, there are a significant number of such children in Key Stage 2 classrooms, and the level of provision for their needs is often inadequate.

KEY STAGE 2 READING SATS 1996

READING LEVELS 1–2

At these levels the SAT involves supported reading with a text chosen from a selected list of books which includes some titles from the Key Stage 1 list and the use of Running Record at Level 2.

LEVELS 3–5

Magazine format used to include any combinations of the following:
• *narrative* in the form of a short story;
• *non-narrative* texts, for example, information texts, letters of complaint, brochures, advertising material;
• *poetry*.
Reading Answer booklet: children work through the answer booklet which explores the reading strands of the National Curriculum but requires response in the form of writing.

LEVEL 6

Separate test based on three types of text, and questions which focus on reference to a range of reading, critical response, awareness of language features and reflective reading.

There is no indication that the SATs will stay in their present form after 1996, and therefore it would be a much better use of teaching time to focus on the Programmes of Study and beyond, and to let the SATs take their correct place at the end of Key Stage 2.

IMPLICATIONS FOR PRACTICE

A teacher should:
1. *Teach* the Programmes of Study for Reading at Key Stage 2.
2. Ensure that the children are familiar with the *range* of texts outlined in the Orders.
3. Ensure that there is *regular, focused discussion* of stories, poetry and information texts.
4. Towards the end of Key Stage 2, let the children see, discuss and work from previous SAT material.
NB: If you only do '4', then your children will not achieve well

and the status quo will be preserved. The first three points are the most significant.

SUMMARY

The value of teacher assessment cannot be over-stated. It need not be seen as additional to existing systems. Teachers need to review which of their current assessment procedures are worth keeping. If they do not inform planning, are we justified in keeping them? Planning and assessment are inter-related. Clearly identified learning objectives will provide assessment opportunities. Assessment is not then seen as an end in itself, but as the key to effective teaching and learning.

REFERENCES

Arnold, H. (1982) *Listening to Children Reading*, Hodder & Stoughton.

Ashcroft, K. and Palacio, D. (1995) *The Primary Teacher's Guide to the New National Curriculum*, Falmer Press.

Barber, A. and Bailey, D. *The Mousehole Cat*, (1993) Walker Books.

Barrs, M., Ellis, S., Hester, H. and Thomas, A. (eds) (1988) *The Primary Language Record*, CLPE.

Bielby, N. (1994) *Making Sense of Reading*, Scholastic Ltd.

Chambers, A. (1993) *Tell Me*, Thimble Press.

DES The Cox Report (1989) *English from 5 to 16*, HMSO.

DFE The Dearing Report (1993) *The National Curriculum and its Assessment*, HMSO.

Goodman, KS. (ed) (1973) *Miscue Analysis: applications to reading instruction*, ERIC/NCTE, Urbana, Illinois

Lewis, M. and Wray, D. (1994) EXEL publications from Exeter University School of Education.

Lewis, M. and Wray, D. (1995) *Developing Children's Writing*, Primary Professional Bookshelf, Scholastic Ltd.

Littlefair, A. (1991) *Reading All Types of Writing*, Open University Press.

Mallett, M. (1992) *Making Facts Matter: Reading Non-Fiction*, Paul Chapman.

Neate, B. (1992) *Finding Out About Finding Out*, Hodder & Stoughton.

Nimmo, J. (1993) *The Witches and the Singing Mice*, (1993) Picture Lion

Oxfordshire County Council, (1995) *Oxfordshire Reading Record*, OCC.

PAGE–The Primary Advisory Group for English, Oxfordshire County Council, (1993) *Oxfordshire Curriculum Matters–Eight Papers on the Teaching of Reading*, OCC.

SCAA (1995) *Consistency in Teacher Assessment. Exemplification of Standards: English: Key Stages 1 & 2, Levels 1-5 Reading, Writing*, SCAA.

SCAA (1994) *Key Stage 2 National Pilot: English Teachers' Guide*, SCAA.

SCAA (1995) *Key Stage 1 English Tasks 1996, Reading and Writing Teacher's Handbook*, SCAA.

FURTHER READING

Barrs, M. *et al.* (1988) *The Primary Language Record*, CLPE.

Barrs, M and Thomas, A. (Eds) *The Reading Book*, CLPE.

Bryant, P. and Bradley, L. (1985) *Children's Reading Problems*, Blackwell.

Chambers, A. (1985) *Booktalk*, The Bodley Head.

Davies, P., Karavis, S., Monk, J. (1993) 'Becoming a reader', (three articles) in *Language and Learning*, Questions.

Goswami, U. and Bryant, P. (1990) *Phonological Skills and Learning to Read*, Lawrence Erlbaum Associates Ltd.

Karavis, S. and Davies, P. (1995) *Progress in English: Assessment and Record-keeping at KS 1 and 2*, Reading and Language Information Centre, University of Reading.

Oldham, S. (1994) *How can Booktalk be effectively implemented to develop reflective reading*, unpublished dissertation Westminster College, Oxford.

Perera, K. (1984) *Children's Writing and Reading: Analysing Classroom Language*, Blackwell.

White, J. and Karavis, S. *et al.* (1994) *The Reading Repertoire at Key Stage 2*, NFER.

TESTS REFERRED TO IN TEXT

Cloze Reading Tests, Young, D. (1992) Hodder & Stoughton.

Diagnostic Reading Record, Arnold, H. (1992) Hodder & Stoughton.

Edinburgh Reading Tests, The Godfrey Thompson Unit, University of Edinburgh, (1977) Hodder & Stoughton.

Effective Reading Tests, Vincent, D. and de la Mare, M. (1986) NFER.

Group Reading Test Young, D. (1992) Hodder & Stoughton.

Holborn Sentence Reading Test

Neale Analysis of Reading Ability, Neale, M. D. (1988) NFER.

Salford Sentence Reading Test, Bookbinder, G. E. (1976) Hodder & Stoughton.

Schonell Graded Word Reading Test, Schonell, F. (1945) Oliver & Boyd.

Word Search, The Godfrey Thomson Unit, University of Edinburgh (1986) Hodder & Stoughton.

INDEX